THE 28 DAY PLAN

THE 28 DAY PLAN

Christine Green

p

This is a Parragon Book

This editon published in 2003

Parragon
Queen Street House
4 Queen Street
Bath BA1 1HE, UK

Copyright © Parragon 2002

Designed, produced and packaged by
Stonecastle Graphics Limited

Text by Christine Green
Edited by Gillian Haslam
Designed by Sue Pressley and Paul Turner
Commissioned photography by Roddy Paine

ISBN 1-40541-034-5

Printed in China

Disclaimer

The exercises and advice detailed in this book
assume that you are a normally healthy adult.
Therefore the author, publishers, their servants or
agents cannot accept responsibility for loss or
damage suffered by individuals as a result of
following advice or attempting an exercise or
treatment referred to in this book. It is strongly
recommended that individuals intending to
undertake an exercise programme and any
change of diet do so following consultation with
their doctor.

Introduction

If you feel tired all the time, think you could benefit from losing a few kilograms
or wish to tone up your body, then this book is the answer to your prayers – whether you
are looking for a complete body overhaul or a few pointers to a healthier lifestyle.

The six sections in this book each contain an easy-to-use 28-day plan. If you feel lacking in energy, follow the energize programme or the 28-day detox plan. There is a daily plan for banishing cellulite and another for getting your body in shape for summer. There is a four-week programme for toning up your hips and thighs, and another plan to show you the way to achieve an enviably flat stomach.

The plans can be followed in which order you choose, and each contains week-by-week schedules you can adapt to suit your own lifestyle. There are simple recipes and advice on healthy eating, easy exercise regimes to practise at home or in the gym, plus masses of ideas for pampering both body and soul. So follow the advice and suggestions given here and soon you will see a new 'you'.

Contents

The 28 Day Plan

DETOX

What is Detoxification?

Imagine a well-toned body, the loss of several kilograms of weight, healthy skin, increased energy, better digestion. You feel fit and healthy and able to relax at the drop of a hat – does it sound too good to be true?

Don't despair – it is possible and it is achievable on a 28-day detox programme following which you will feel so much healthier, more energetic, cleansed and revitalized!

Detoxing is not a diet nor is it a strict eating regime. Just as you would spring-clean your home, when you detox you are in effect spring-cleaning your body, clearing out all the toxins and poisons that have accumulated inside you over the years. Toxins enter the body in many ways – from the air we breathe to the food we eat, from pollutants in the environment to the emotional stresses of everyday life, all these factors can contribute to toxic build-up. After a while they can knock the body off balance, leaving you feeling sluggish and lacking in energy. However, it is possible to eliminate those toxins, to bring the body back into balance and to return it to good health by detoxing. In doing so you are:

✓ Improving your immune system
✓ Improving your circulation
✓ Ensuring the body has all the necessary energy it requires to 'look after and repair' itself

How does it work?

The body is a complex machine and, like any machine, it needs regular maintenance to keep it working efficiently. The body needs a daily intake of fluid and food to provide it with energy, to keep it healthy and to help repair and renew damaged cells. Food is processed by the body's metabolism. Once the internal

Signs of possible toxic overload
- Allergic reactions
- Bloating and sweating
- Constant tiredness
- Headaches
- Intolerance to fat
- Mood changes
- Poor concentration
- Poor digestion

organs have extracted the nutrients from the foods, the rest is simply waste and is transported to those organs whose role it is to eliminate waste products from the body.

Liver: This organ has many important functions, one of which is to transport unwanted or toxic substances that enter the body and to transform them into substances that the body can either retain or expel.

Kidneys: These filter and eliminate toxins from the blood via the urine. They also ensure that the body has sufficient fluid and that the balance of potassium and sodium, both important elements for regulating the amount of fluids in the body, is maintained.

Lymphatic system: Acting as a waste disposal unit, the lymphatic system is a network of vessels extending all around the body. It produces a liquid called lymph that absorbs micro-organisms, dead cells, excess fluids and other waste products derived from food. It transports them to the lymph nodes where the fluid is filtered, taken into the bloodstream and on to eliminatory organs where unwanted substances are expelled from the body via urine, faeces or sweat.

Skin: An important indicator as to what is happening

How to succeed on the programme
✓ Adopt a positive attitude from the beginning
✓ Stay focused – remember why you are doing it
✓ Regard each day as a new challenge
✓ Keep it exciting by adding different treatments
✓ Experiment with different foods
✓ And don't forget, pamper yourself

Following the detox programme

The greatest attraction about detoxing is the 'good-to-be-alive/full-of-energy/I'm raring-to-go' feeling that it produces. Ask anyone who has followed a detox programme and they will almost certainly agree that they felt fitter after it than they had done in years. Age is not important – you may be 25 or 55, a full-time housewife or a busy employee climbing up the executive ladder. The simple fact is that we all get stressed, we all rush around too much and we all tend to eat more convenience food than perhaps we should. Can you imagine how our insides must look? The answer is to detox in order to restore inner cleanliness. The results will be amazing, but you must be determined. You'll need a good helping of willpower to complete the recommended programme.

within our body and the overall state of our health. As an organ, it excretes large quantities of waste, such as urea, salts, uric acid, ammonia and water.

If these organs do not work efficiently, our long-term health will invariably suffer and the body will not be able to repair itself following stress or illness. The organs slow down, and the accumulation of waste and toxins builds up to such an extent that toxic overload becomes almost inevitable. This throws the body out of balance, and the only way to restore balance is by following a detoxification programme to cleanse the system.

You are not advised to go on a detox programme if:
• You are pregnant or breastfeeding
• You are seeing a doctor for a medical condition
• You have Type 1 diabetes
• You have anaemia
• You are underweight
• You are under stress
• You are taking prescription medicines that should not be discontinued

It is always recommended that you check with your doctor or practice nurse before going on a detox programme.

Healthy Eating

The basic principle of our detox programme is to eat three well-chosen meals a day – breakfast, lunch and dinner – allowing at least five hours between them to allow the body enough time to process the food before the next meal.

If possible, try to eat the last meal of the day no later than 7.00pm; this gives the body ample time to digest the food before you go to bed.

Choosing what to eat is half the fun of the programme. While it is very specific in the sense that if foods are not listed, they should not be eaten, there are so many delicious dishes that are recommended that you will be spoiled for choice.

But do not worry if your culinary skills are not quite up to cordon bleu standard, don't worry; it is amazing how different a salad can taste with the addition of some herbs or a few nuts sprinkled over the top.

Fresh fruit and vegetables are a major part of the detox programme, largely because of the abundance of minerals and vitamins that they contain. Canned and processed foods are best avoided as they contain additives and preservatives. However, if you do find yourself having to eat some, make sure that most of that meal is salad or lightly steamed vegetables.

Recommended fruit

- Apples
- Apricots
- Bilberries
- Blackberries
- Blackcurrants
- Blueberries
- Cherries
- Cranberries
- Currants
- Damsons
- Dates
- Figs
- Gooseberries
- Grapefruit
- Grapes
- Greengages
- Guavas
- Kiwi fruit
- Lemons
- Limes
- Loganberries
- Lychees
- Mangoes
- Melons
- Mulberries
- Nectarines
- Passionfruit
- Paw-paw
- Peaches
- Pears
- Pineapple
- Plums
- Pomegranates
- Prunes
- Quinces
- Raisins
- Raspberries
- Redcurrants
- Rhubarb
- Strawberries
- Sultanas

Recommended vegetables

- Artichokes
- Asparagus
- Aubergines
- Beans (broad, butter, French, haricot, mung, red kidney, runner)
- Beansprouts
- Beetroot
- Broccoli
- Brussels sprouts
- Cabbage (red, savoy, spring, white, winter)
- Carrots
- Cauliflower
- Celeriac
- Celery
- Chicory
- Chinese leaf
- Courgettes
- Cucumbers
- Fennel
- Kohlrabi
- Leeks
- Lettuce
- Marrows
- Okra
- Onions
- Parsnips
- Peas
- Peppers (bell, capsicum)
- Plantain
- Potatoes
- Pumpkins
- Radishes
- Spring greens
- Spring onions
- Swede
- Sweetcorn
- Sweet potatoes
- Squashes
- Turnips
- Watercress
- Yams

Recommended nuts

High in calories, nuts are also high in fibre, nutrients and potassium so are an ideal source of unsaturated fatty acids. Best eaten raw, unsalted and fresh. Choose from the following:

- Almonds
- Brazils
- Cashews
- Chestnuts
- Hazelnuts
- Macadamia
- Pecans
- Pine nuts
- Pistachios
- Walnuts

Recommended seeds, pulses and herbs

Just as nuts are high in nutrients, so too are pulses and seeds. Once fully sprouted, their nutrient content becomes higher. Great for adding flavour and colour to foods.

Pulses and seeds:
- Alfalfa
- Cardamom pods
- Chickpeas
- Chillies
- Pumpkin seeds
- Sesame seeds
- Sunflower seeds

Herbs:
- Cayenne pepper
- Basil
- Coriander
- Dill
- Fennel
- Ginger
- Lemon grass
- Marjoram
- Parsley
- Pepper
- Rosemary
- Sage
- Tarragon
- Thyme

Recommended fish

Fish is a perfect food as it contains all the vital proteins. As with most food, it is healthier if eaten fresh rather than frozen; freezing depletes fish of many of its essential nutrients. Smoked fish is fine provided it has been treated naturally. Avoid eating fish in brine – it is too salty. If selecting canned fish, those preserved in olive or vegetable oil are the best.

- Cod
- Crab
- Haddock
- Halibut
- Herring
- Lemon sole
- Lobster
- Mackerel
- Monkfish
- Pilchards
- Plaice
- Prawns
- Salmon
- Sardines
- Shrimps
- Skate
- Trout
- Tuna

Foods to avoid
- Artificial sweeteners
- Avocados
- Bananas
- Bread
- Cow's milk/cheese
- Food additives or preservatives
- Lentils
- Mushrooms
- Oranges
- Red meat
- Salt
- Spinach
- Sugar
- Tomatoes

Other recommended foods

Other foods that are important in your detox programme and that can help to add flavour to meals include:

- Balsamic vinegar
- Cider vinegar
- Grapeseed oil
- Miso mustard
- Olive oil
- Olives
- Quorn
- Rice cakes
- Seaweed
- Sesame oil
- Tahini
- Tofu
- Walnut oil

If you cannot find them in your supermarket, then most health food stores will stock them.

Recommended non-dairy products

- Goat's milk/cheese/yogurt
- Sheep's milk/cheese/yogurt
- Rice milk
- Soya milk

Healthy Drinking

Maintaining a healthy balance of fluids is always essential, especially when you consider that the body is made up of 80 per cent water, but when detoxing it is particularly important to increase your intake of fluid to help cleanse the system and flush out any impurities.

Fruit juices: These can be drunk in addition to the recommended quantity of water. If buying pre-packed, check the label that it is pure, unsweetened juice and not the variety made up in water from fruit pulp. Better still, if you have a juicer make your own.

Apple juice
275g (10oz) or 2 medium-sized hard apples

There is no need to peel the apple, simply chop it up roughly and pop the pieces into the juicer. Rich in vitamin C, this is an excellent liver and kidney cleanser and assists the growth and development of a healthy nervous system.

Water: Your aim must be to drink at least 1.75 litres (3 pints) of water a day. That may seem a lot and likely to cause several unscheduled visits to the loo, but after several days the body will adjust. And if drinking plain water becomes a little boring, try adding lemon, lime, honey or ginger to flavour it.
Herbal teas: Echinacea and fenugreek are reputedly the best.
Dandelion coffee: Available from health food shops, this is sometimes drunk as an alternative to coffee.

Home-made fruit juices to try
If you have a juicer, you can make your own fresh juice using any of the following fruits:

- Apples
- Grapes
- Grapefruit
- Lemons
- Limes
- Mango
- Melons
- Papaya
- Peaches
- Pears
- Pineapple
- Strawberries
- Watermelon

Grapefruit juice

275g (10oz) or 1¹/₂ grapefruits

The pink ones are great for this as they are slightly sweeter than other types. Peel off the skin but leave on the pith. Chop up the fruit roughly and then put the pieces into the juicer. Grapefruit contains pectin which can help to lower blood cholesterol and half a grapefruit provides more than half the daily requirement of vitamin C.

Peach juice

350g (12oz) or 2 medium-sized peaches

Leave the skin on, cut the fruit in half, remove the stone and then put it into the juicer. Peach juice is ideal for helping to cleanse the intestines and colon. It also helps to regulate blood fat levels, maintains healthy skin and assists in the healing of wounds.

Home-made vegetable juices

Some vegetables can also be juiced successfully. The choice is varied, but beetroot, carrot, celery, cucumber and watercress all make delicious drinks and are full of vitamins.

Drinks to avoid
- Alcohol and fizzy drinks
- Hot chocolate
- Tea • Coffee

Carrot juice

400g (14oz) or 3 large carrots

With a slightly spicy taste, carrot juice can be made extra tasty by adding some freshly chopped herbs. Simply wash and slice the carrots, and pop them into the juicer. Carrot juice is a very good source of fibre and helps to boost immunity. It helps to cleanse the liver of excess fats, aids digestion and is an excellent source of vitamin A.

Beetroot juice

125g (4oz) or ¹/₃ medium-sized beetroot

Raw beetroot is better than cooked beetroot. Wash it thoroughly and remove any roots. Then slice it and put the pieces into the juicer. Beetroot juice is excellent for cleansing the blood and kidneys and aids the development of a healthy nervous system.

Planning What You Can Eat

By changing your eating habits and eating healthy foods regularly, your energy levels will be maintained throughout the day, you will feel more alert and you will not be piling on extra pounds with that mid-morning chocolate bar.

The detox programme is not a diet and so you should serve yourself adequate helpings that each day should include:

- Three portions of vegetables
- Three portions of fruit
- Three portions of salad
- One portion of non-dairy yogurt, cheese or milk
- Two portions of nuts or fish
- One portion of brown rice

The above list may seem a little daunting to you, especially if you generally skip breakfast, grab a quick sandwich for lunch and perhaps rustle up a shepherd's pie for supper.

The best advice when it comes to planning your daily eating schedule is to draw up some menus a week in advance so that you will know what you are eating for breakfast, lunch and dinner on each of the days ahead.

Methods of cooking

If cooking is not your forte, then you will love the detox programme because there is practically no cooking involved! In general, the less food is heated, the more nutrients it will retain. Of course, there are exceptions, such as fish which must be thoroughly cooked. If you prefer your vegetables slightly cooked, then avoid boiling, slow-cooking or frying them; use other methods, such as stir frying, grilling or just pop them into the microwave – these are far tastier and less likely to impair the natural flavour and nutrients in the food.

While on the programme make sure each day you:

✓ Drink a cup of hot water containing lemon or lime juice each morning
✓ Drink at least 1.75 litres (3 pints) of water
✓ Take two liver tonics
✓ Take two kidney tonics
✓ Take a kelp supplement
✓ Take a multivitamin supplement for the first 15 days
✓ Eat three meals a day
✓ Eat one portion of rice (preferably brown short grain)
✓ Eat three portions of vegetables (one of which should be raw)
✓ Eat three portions of fruit
✓ Eat three portions of fresh salad
✓ Eat one portion of a non-dairy product

Calorie intake

All foods contain calories which are a measure of the amount of energy contained in that particular food. The number of calories your body requires each day largely depends on your age, lifestyle, etc. The general consensus is that the average woman needs approximately 1600 calories per day. If the calorie intake is reduced to lower than 1000, then the body is not getting enough to function properly and will begin to go into starvation mode.

Daily Treatments

To achieve the goal of the detox programme – a cleansed inner body and an invigorated
spirit – it is important that you follow the recommendations on page 17
throughout your 28-day plan.

Why certain foods are important

Hot lemon water: Starting the day with a cup of hot
water and a squeeze of lemon or lime juice will
freshen your mouth and give a kick-start to your liver
(the largest organ involved in detoxing).

Water: Cleansing, restoring and rejuvenating the body
are the three basic principles of a detox programme
and the one vital ingredient which can help is water.
So make sure you drink plenty of it.

Liver tonic: The liver should be treated with kid gloves
throughout the 28-day programme so that it does its
job of detoxification efficiently. To help do this, it
needs a tonic in the shape of at least two of the
following foods each day:

• Two cups of fennel or dandelion tea
• A medium-sized glass of pure carrot or beetroot juice
• Eat a medium-sized bunch of grapes
• Include a fresh clove of garlic in your food

Kidney tonic: Like the liver, the kidneys have a hard
job to do in detoxing the system. Including certain
foods in your diet will enable them to work more
efficiently. Each day follow two of these suggestions:

• Sip a teaspoon of fresh honey dissolved in a cup of
hot water
• Drink a medium-sized glass of freshly squeezed
cranberry juice
• Eat half a medium-sized melon

Supplements: When you change your eating habits
significantly, your metabolic rate is often affected; if
sufficient quantities of foods are not consumed, the
body begins slowing down. At the start of your
programme, you may find it helpful to take certain
supplements, such as kelp which equips the body with
enough iodine to balance the metabolism.

Vitamin supplements: It is often a good idea to
include an all-round vitamin supplement in the initial
stages of your detox programme to ensure that the
body is not being depleted of any essential nutrients.
Generally the body adjusts after two weeks of the
programme and you can stop taking the supplements.

Each day throughout your detox programme:
✓ Take a cold shower/bath
✓ Do some self-massage
✓ Perform 30 minutes of exercises
✓ Spend five minutes on quality breathing
✓ Spend ten minutes enjoying some relaxation
✓ Do five minutes of visualization exercises
✓ Smile or laugh heartily every day
✓ Exfoliate every three days
✓ Take an Epsom salts bath every five days

T.L.C. (Tender Loving Care)

The detox programme can only really be hailed as a success if the entire 'person', inside and outside, has been cleansed and restored. This is where a combination of exercise, relaxation and pampering comes in.

The benefits of a cold shower

Refreshing, invigorating and rejuvenating, a morning shower is just what the body needs to jump-start it into action. But when you are nearly finished, gradually turn on the cold tap allowing cold water to run over your body for one minute. This might sound uncomfortable but that minute of cold water will:

✓ tone up the skin

✓ tone up the muscles

✓ give the lymphatic system a jump-start

If you don't have a shower, then simply take a bath as usual and, as the water drains away, turn the cold water on, gather it in your cupped hands and splash it over your body. Better still, if you have a shower attachment that you can fit over the cold water tap, use this to spray yourself with cold water.

Self-massage

There is nothing quite like a full body massage to relieve tension, lower blood pressure and stress levels, eliminate excess fluids and toxins and give the skin an overall healthy glow. It can be expensive going to a beauty salon, so why not bring the beauty salon to your home and do it yourself? If you have a willing partner to help you, so much the better, otherwise try giving yourself this very simple head massage, ideal for dealing with a tension headache. A five-minute massage will leave you feeling totally relaxed.

1. Begin by taking several deep breaths.

2. Using the thumb and forefinger of each hand, very gently pinch your earlobes and massage the edges of the ears moving all the way round up to the top and pulling them slightly away from the head.

3. Now move on to massage the temples using the first two fingers of each hand.

4. Finally concentrate on the top of the head and apply firm pressure all over the scalp, almost as if you were washing your hair.

Skin brushing

No-one had ever heard of dry skin brushing a few years ago, but now it is one of the 'in things' to do. It helps to clean the skin of all the dead cells that clog up the pores, leaving the skin soft and smooth. But that's not all it does. A gentle five-minute daily skin brush is an effective, simple way to boost the lymphatic system. It is also excellent for helping to eliminate most women's number one enemy – cellulite!

How to skin brush

• Take a natural bristle brush or a dry flannel, begin at the feet and, using small circular strokes, gradually move up the body always brushing towards the heart with gentle, long and firm movements.

• Never brush away from the heart, this may cause faintness or unsettle the natural flow of the blood.

• Keep each stroke firm as you work your way gradually up the body from the ankles to the knees, from the knees to the top of your thighs and over your buttocks.

• Starting at the wrists, move up the arms to the shoulders and down from the tops of the arms over the shoulders, then gently up the neck to the base of the skull.

• Work over the stomach using gentle strokes in a clockwise direction to prevent upsetting the digestive flow in your intestines. Be extra gentle on the breasts and avoid brushing over the nipples.

• Don't expect to notice changes after the first treatment but once you have done it several times, your skin will begin to feel softer and smoother.

Exercise and Relaxation

Exercise is the ideal way to get the body system going and to increase the metabolic rate.
Some exercises are better suited to the detox programme than others.

Walking

Gentle and easy, walking stimulates the heart, lungs, muscles and mind. Begin with 10-15 minutes each day, gradually building up to 30 minutes. Walk fast enough to work up a slight sweat.

Swimming

Swimming works most of the major muscle groups and is an excellent aerobic exercise. Check if there are any classes at your local pool.

Cycling

This is one of the best types of exercise for building muscular endurance and toning up leg muscles. If you don't own a real bike, the same benefits can be derived from an exercise bike – a good reason to join a local gym!

If you haven't exercised for a while:
- Don't exercise too strenuously to begin with – overtired muscles create waste products and put a strain on the lymphatic system
- Whatever exercise you decide to do, begin slowly and then build up gradually
- Don't push yourself too hard
- Try to find an exercise that frees the mind
- Don't choose something you don't like – remember exercise should be enjoyable

Bouncing

Bouncing on a 'mini trampoline' for 5–15 minutes daily is perfect for helping to drain the lymphatic system.

Housework

It's official – a vigorous burst of housework can be as good for you as a trip to the gym, and scrubbing the floor burns up 400 calories an hour! So if you are concerned that your house is getting neglected while you are on the programme, you could always integrate housework as one form of exercise. The secret is to do a job in half the time you would normally take, putting the maximum amount of effort in!

Exercise is good for you and it should also be fun. Set some time aside to enjoy an invigorating bike ride or play some favourite music and bounce on a mini trampoline in time with the rhythm.

Breathing

Another important element in your detox programme is to spend at least five minutes each day on quality deep breathing. Very few of us breathe correctly and whenever we feel tense or worried, our breathing pattern becomes shallow and chest movements erratic. Correct breathing will rectify this. This is the art of deep breathing:

Why learning to breathe correctly is important:
- It helps to cleanse the body
- It teaches you how to relax
- It energizes your body

1. Lie down on the floor in a quiet room.
2. Place both hands on your abdomen, fingertips gently touching.
3. Slowly begin to breathe in through your nose to the count of four.
4. Hold for a few seconds and then, as you exhale to the count of eight, become aware of your stomach expanding and your fingertips parting.
5. Practise this sequence several times.

To begin with it will feel rather strange but persevere and soon you will begin to feel more relaxed and there will be no need to use your fingers to check that your abdomen (rather than your chest) is expanding.

Relaxation

Breathing correctly acts as a natural tranquilliser for the nervous system and so the deeper you breathe, the calmer the mind becomes. Acquiring the ability to relax totally is something very few people achieve but the benefits of practising relaxation techniques can stand you in good stead for coping with most of life's day-to-day stresses.

Standing in a supermarket queue or waiting in a traffic jam will not seem so irritating once you have learned some simple relaxation exercises. That's not to say you won't have the odd lapse now and again nor that you will always feel calm and together, but it will at least demonstrate that a relaxed state of mind is achievable with a little practice.

Follow these simple steps and don't be surprised if you end up falling asleep!

1. Lie down on a comfortable mat in a quiet room, legs outstretched, arms resting gently by your sides.

2. Close your eyes and take a few slow, deep breaths.

3. As you inhale, tense all the muscles in your body, feel them tighten and become taut. Then, as you exhale, become aware of all the tension ebbing away.

4. Bring your shoulders up to your ears as far as you can, making sure that your head stays flat on the mat, count to five and then slowly drop your shoulders back to their original position.

5. Now for your arms. Tense them; as you do so they will automatically draw in nearer to your body, hold for a count of five, and then release. Become aware of the tension ebbing away as your arms fall limply to either side of your body.

6. Then repeat the tension and relaxation sequence with your abdomen, buttocks, legs and feet.

Visualization

Five minutes spent totally submerged in a pleasant make-believe world can be five of the most valuable minutes in your detox programme. It is all a matter of concentration.

The objective is to sit back, close your eyes and imagine yourself in any situation which makes you feel happy: lying on a warm beach with the sun beating down, sitting in a field on a bright summer's day, take whatever mental image is a good, positive one for you. Linger over as many details as you are sure in making the image come alive. Then, as often as possible, bring this picture to the forefront of your mind keeping the thoughts that are associated with the picture positive and full of energy.

These images or visualizations are ways of helping to see yourself attaining goals and achieving success. When you have been practising them for a while, you will start to gain confidence and think more positively about yourself.

climb back into the bath and carry on rubbing until all the cream has been washed off.

4. Get out of the bath and towel yourself dry before applying moisturizer all over your body.

5. Finally jump into a pair of your warmest pyjamas, and hop into bed with a good book for a restorative early night.

Epsom salts baths

Speed up the elimination of toxins from the skin and improve your circulation with an Epsom salts bath. Run the bath water and add 225-450g ($^1/_2$-1lb) of Epsom salts to the water. Most chemists and health food stores sell Epsom salts.

Soak for about 20 minutes, and when you get out, keep yourself warm by piling on lots clothes; this will help the body to continue sweating out toxins.

Laughter

Can you remember the last time you had a jolly good laugh or was it so long ago, you've forgotten?

Experts have found that people who use humour to cope with stress experience:

- ✓ Less tension
- ✓ Less fatigue
- ✓ Less anger
- ✓ Less depression

And, furthermore, laughing:

- ✓ Relaxes face muscles
- ✓ Exercises internal muscles
- ✓ Deepens breathing
- ✓ Improves blood circulation
- ✓ Lowers blood pressure and releases endorphins, the feel-good chemicals that are the body's natural painkillers

So hire a comedy video, read a funny book or watch your favourite TV sitcom and have a good laugh.

Exfoliate

Every day exfoliate the skin. Not unlike dry skin brushing, exfoliation clears the skin of dead cells; the main difference is that it needs to be done with water and an exfoliater, so this treatment could easily be integrated with one of your pampering sessions.

1. As you run a bath, add a few drops of your favourite bath oil and relax for at least ten minutes in the water, allowing time for your skin to soften before you begin to exfoliate.

2. You can either apply exfoliation cream while in the bath, lifting each limb out of the water to do so, or climb out of the bath and apply the cream using firm circular movements all over your body. When finished,

Good Food

The great thing about the detox programme is that it gives you the opportunity to have fun and experiment with a range of different foods.

Use your imagination and create some dishes that may well become a staple part of your diet long after the programme has ended. If you are looking for some ideas, here are a few to tempt you.

Breakfast recipes

It's essential to have breakfast and here are some tasty recipes which are quick and easy to prepare.

Pear delight

1 glass apple juice
1 pear
150ml (5fl oz) goat's or sheep's milk yogurt

Peel the pear and place it in a pan with the apple juice and some water. Bring to the boil and simmer until the pear has softened. Place the pear in a breakfast bowl and pour the yogurt over it.

Muesli

Oats
Raisins
Sesame seeds
Hazelnuts
Sunflower seeds
Sheep's milk yogurt

Simply mix two dessertspoons of each dry ingredient in a bowl and soak them overnight in enough water to make the mixture slightly moist. In the morning serve with sheep's milk yogurt.

Porridge

Jumbo porridge oats
Water
Handful of raisins

Put the oats into the bowl and stir in some water to the desired consistency. Then add a handful of raisins for sweetness.

Oats

Raw oats
$1/2$ chopped apple
1-2 tablespoons raisins
$1/2$ teaspoon cinnamon
Tablespoon raw honey

Put quarter of a cup of raw unprocessed oats in a dish with some distilled water and leave overnight to soak. The next morning add the remaining ingredients, stir and enjoy.

Lunchtime recipes

These suggestions are quick to prepare, and provide something light but nutritious and healthy to keep you going until your evening meal.

Potato salad

Portion cooked new potatoes
1 red onion, chopped
Lemon juice
Olive oil
1 tablespoon pine nuts
Portion cooked prawns
1 fennel bulb, chopped

Cook the new potatoes in a pan of boiling water. When almost cooked, drain and slice each in half. Fry the chopped onion and fennel in the olive oil until translucent. Add the potato halves and fry until everything is slightly browned. While browning the vegetables, lightly toast the pine nuts. When the vegetables are almost done, add the prawns and pine nuts, cook for a further 2 minutes. Toss the whole salad together and dress with a drizzle of fresh lemon juice.

Rice salad

$1/2$ green pepper, deseeded and cored
$1/2$ red pepper, deseeded and cored
5cm (2in) piece of cucumber
60g (2oz) boiled brown rice, rinsed and drained
30g (1oz) cooked peas
30g (1oz) cooked sweetcorn
Soy sauce
Black pepper
Pinch of salt

Chop the peppers and cucumber very finely and mix in with the rice, peas and sweetcorn. Add the soy sauce and season to taste.

Jacket potato
1 large potato
Olive oil
Portion fresh tuna
2 small chicory bulbs
Balsamic vinegar

Bake the potato until soft. Pre-heat the grill. Drizzle a little olive oil over a piece of fresh tuna and grill until it begins to turn light brown. Slice the chicory, place strips on top of the tuna and brown under the grill for the last few minutes. Make a dressing from two teaspoons of olive oil and some balsamic vinegar to taste. Serve the tuna with the jacket potato, pouring the dressing over the fish.

Watercress soup
Enough for two or three servings.
900ml (1¹/₂ pints) vegetable stock
1 large onion, finely chopped
1 clove garlic, crushed
450g (1 lb) potatoes, scrubbed and cubed
Large pinch mixed dried herbs
Sea salt
Freshly ground black pepper
Bunch watercress, washed and chopped

Heat 3-4 tablespoons of the vegetable stock in a large saucepan. Add the onion, garlic and potatoes. Cook on a medium heat for 5 minutes, then bring to the boil. Add the herbs, salt and pepper and cook until potatoes are tender (approximately 20 minutes). Add the watercress and cook for a further 5 minutes. Cool slightly, then pour into the liquidizer and blend until smooth. Return to the saucepan, reheat gently, stirring in more of the remaining stock or adding water if the soup is still too thick.

Bean salad
Full of protein and a satisfying lunch to keep those hunger pangs at bay. This recipe makes enough for a family of four.
200g (7oz) can red kidney beans
200g (7oz) can cut green beans
200g (7oz) can chickpeas
200g (7oz) can butter beans
1 red onion, chopped
1 red pepper, deseeded and chopped
3 sticks celery, finely sliced
75g (3oz) sultanas
150ml (5fl oz) sheep's yogurt
Salt and pepper

Drain the beans and chickpeas and place in a large bowl. Add the onion, pepper, celery and sultanas, stir in the yogurt and season to taste. If you wish, this can be served with a green salad.

Dinner recipes

The following dishes are perfect either for entertaining guests or to eat as your main meal of the day.

Cod and potato

1 cod steak

2 large potatoes

1 small leek, shredded

1 piece of green cabbage, shredded

1 clove garlic, crushed

Olive oil

Freshly ground black pepper

Peel, chop and boil the potatoes until they are soft. Place the cod under the grill and cook on both sides until slightly golden. Put a small amount of olive oil into a pan and fry the shredded leek, cabbage and garlic until slightly browned. Add a tablespoonful of olive oil to the potatoes and mash until creamy. Place the mashed potato in the centre of a plate, put the grilled cod on top and season with black pepper.

Savoury potatoes

This dish is savoury, tasty and delicious.

5–6 medium-sized new potatoes

Olive oil

1 small onion, sliced

1 small fennel bulb, sliced

1–2 sprigs of rosemary

2 cloves garlic, crushed

1 small courgette, sliced

1 tablespoon lemon juice

Fresh basil and coriander, chopped

Boil the new potatoes until soft. Heat three tablespoons of olive oil in the pan and fry the onion, fennel and rosemary until they are soft and lightly browned. Drain the potatoes and add them to the frying pan. Add the garlic and courgette and fry for 10 minutes until the potatoes are browned. Remove from the heat, add the lemon juice, basil and coriander, remove the rosemary and serve.

Vegetable bake

3 medium onions, chopped

3-4 carrots, diced

2 large potatoes, peeled and sliced

300ml (10fl oz) vegetable stock

2 teaspoons dried mint

1 tablespoon olive oil

2 cloves garlic, crushed

Sea salt

Freshly ground black pepper

1 tablespoon sesame seeds

Preheat the oven to 400°F/200°C/gas mark 6. Place the onions, carrots and potatoes in a saucepan with the vegetable stock. Bring to the boil then simmer for about 15 minutes. Lightly oil a casserole dish and pour the onions, carrots and stock from the saucepan in it, plus the mint and seasoning. Layer the sliced potatoes over the top with garlic and sesame seeds sprinkled over and pop in the oven for approximately 30 minutes or until the potatoes turn golden brown.

Delicious desserts

Apple surprise

1 large eating apple
Mixture of cherries, raspberries, strawberries
1 tablespoon honey, plus 1 extra teaspoon
1 tablespoon sheep's milk yogurt
Sesame seeds, toasted

Peel and core the apple, place it in a pan with a small
amount of water and steam gently until the fruit is
tender. In a separate pan, simmer the soft fruits with
the honey until they are soft. Place the apple
on a plate, top with the summer fruits
and pour the honey and juice over.
Top with a tablespoonful of yogurt
mixed with a teaspoon of honey
and sprinkle with sesame seeds.

Fruit ice

Handful each of raspberries, blackcurrants
and strawberries
1 tablespoon honey
1 small pot of sheep's yogurt

Remove stalks from the fruit and simmer very gently
in a saucepan with the honey until soft. Transfer the
mixture to a bowl and leave to cool. When cool, put
the bowl into the freezer. Keep checking and just
before it is almost frozen, remove from the freezer.
Pour the yogurt into a blender and gradually spoon in
the fruit. Blend in short bursts as the mixture is
added. Serve straight away or
return to the freezer
for a short while.

Strawberry delight

2 small pots goat's milk yogurt
10 large strawberries

Hull the strawberries and put them
in a blender. Add the yogurt and
blend into a delicious
smoothy. Easy!

Safe snacking

One of the biggest problems when following any new
diet is that you have to change eating habits. Whereas
you may normally grab a quick sandwich at lunchtime
or meet up with friends for a coffee and a cake, you
now have to be prepared to do things differently.

The one thing to remember on the detox
programme is not to skip meals. Be prepared. If you
are going out, for instance take along some of your
own snack foods, a bag of dried fruit or a rice cake.
If you find that you are peckish midway through the
afternoon and are tempted to raid the biscuit tin,
don't. Have a piece of fresh fruit instead or make
yourself a cup of herbal tea.

Work: Most businesses and offices with canteen
facilities cater for a wide variety of diets, so you
should find something to suit you. Alternatively, you
can take something with you and ask a member of

the canteen staff to pop it in the microwave at lunchtime.

Shopping: If you have arranged to meet up with friends in town, there are plenty of places where you can enjoy a jacket potato or a light salad. You could ask for a glass of hot water or herbal tea to drink.

Dining out: There may well be occasions when you are on your detox programme when you want to go out for a meal with friends. Whether you are dining in a high-class restaurant or a corner bistro, most establishments are only too willing to accommodate special requests and make up some alternative dishes.

And if you are eating in a Chinese or Indian restaurant where vegetable dishes tend to be highly spiced, select a suitable main dish and perhaps ask for a portion of plain boiled rice. Never be afraid to ask.

Snacks

Although you should never feel really hungry while on the detox programme, there are bound to be days when you do feel peckish. Don't be tempted to dive into the biscuit tin – there are lots of other alternatives from which you can choose:

✓ Rice cakes (non-salted)
✓ Piece of fresh fruit
✓ Handful of nuts and seeds
✓ Hummus

Remember while on the detox programme:
- Never miss a meal
- If you are out, be prepared and take along something to eat, perhaps dried fruit and nuts stored in a plastic bag
- Remember to tell your friends that you are on a detox programme
- If dining out, don't be afraid to ask the kitchen staff to make you up a salad

Maintaining The Detox

There are bound to be times during the 28-day detox programme when you will feel like giving it all up. These negative thoughts are only to be expected; ignore them, after all they are only thoughts.

To buck yourself up, consider adding some extra rewards into your programme. You might treat yourself to a pedicure, take yourself off to the shops and buy yourself a small gift, write yourself a letter of encouragement and put it in the back of your diary to read when the programme is over, or relax and listen to some favourite music.

Why not take an aromatherapy bath adding some drops of essential oils to the water that will help boost the elimination of toxins and make you feel relaxed? Six drops of your favourite oil are all you need, and a 20-minute soak will rejuvenate and energize you.

Facial scrub

To clear your complexion, improve the circulation and tone up slack muscles, try giving yourself a gentle facial scrub. Apply it with small circular movements over the face and neck before rinsing off with warm water.

Facial scrub for dry skin: Blend one tablespoon of ground almonds with clear honey to form a paste. Apply it over the face and then rinse off with tepid water.
Facial scrub for normal skin: Mix one tablespoon of wheatgerm and one tablespoon of single cream together in a basin until they form a paste. Then massage it gently over the skin and rinse away with tepid water.

Relaxing oils
camomile • lavender • sandalwood • ylang ylang
Revitalizing oils
geranium • grapefruit • lemon • lime
Soothing oils
juniper • lavender • marjoram • rosemary

Facial scrub for oily skin: Add one tablespoon of sugar to the soap lather and apply it when washing the face. Rinse with tepid water.

Some herbs to add to your facial sauna:
Camomile – soothing and cool
Fennel – stimulating and soothing
Geranium – healing and rejuvenating
Lavender – the flowers and leaves are antiseptic
Lemon balm – soothing and astringent

Health problems

It is worth pointing out that you may experience a few health problems while the body is detoxing. Don't worry – this is just nature's way of cleansing the body and ridding it of toxins. They generally clear up by themselves but if symptoms persist or you really don't feel well, then see your doctor. Don't ignore what your body is telling you. Some of the more common problems are:

Constipation: A change in diet nearly always has some effect on the bowels; it should not persist for more than a couple of days. Stools may also be looser than usual due to an increased intake of fibre.

Flu symptoms: Possibly the result of the change in diet. If they are still apparent ten days into the programme, check what you are eating and make sure that you are not overdoing exercise.

Fuzzy tongue: Demonstrating that the body is eliminating toxins.

Headache: The result of caffeine and other chemicals being eliminated from the body.

Spots: The skin is the body's biggest organ of elimination and so spots are very common during a detox programme.

Tiredness: The first few days will be hard as the body adjusts to your new diet. As you persevere, you will begin to feel more energetic. If your energy levels continue to seem depleted, you may not be eating enough.

Facial sauna

A facial sauna is a wonderful way to cleanse and relax the skin, encourage the release of nutrients and eliminate toxins from your skin. For an extra treat add some of your favourite herbs.

1. Remove any make-up and tie your hair back.

2. Boil a pan of water and pour it into a heatproof bowl. If you wish, at this point you can add a handful of your favourite herbs to the water.

3. With a towel draped over your head, lean forward over the bowl, allowing the hot steam to rise and cleanse your face.

4. Remain in the same position for 15 minutes to allow enough time for the pores to open.

After the steam sauna, don't rub or massage your skin. Leave it to dry of its own accord before applying a facemask. If you have thin blood vessels or severe skin blemishes and want to use a facemask to get rid of them, don't use a facial sauna first because it will aggravate the problem.

Detox Days 1–7

Right, the time has come! You've made all your preparations, and you know what the next 28 days hold. The best and most effective way of undertaking the programme is to start on a positive note.

It is good to begin on a Friday as this gives you the weekend to establish a routine. Whether you are a working woman or a busy mother at home, the next 28 days may witness the biggest changes you are ever going to make in your life, so be prepared. Fill in a chart to record each day – you could photocopy the example on page 37 and stick it on your kitchen wall so that you will remember what you must do on each day of the programme.

It's important to keep a diary in which you can record your day's activities, what you ate, how you took time out for yourself, and then at the end of each day make a note of how you felt. Obviously on some days you will find more to write about than others, but by keeping a diary and referring to it when you have negative days, you will keep yourself motivated. You may also wish to keep a record of your weight and measurements using the simple chart on the next page.

Here is a typical plan for the first day but naturally times and the order in which activities are done may differ according to your own lifestyle and some daytime activities can be carried out in the evening when work commitments are over.

7.00am Drink a glass of hot water with a squeeze of fresh lemon or lime juice in it when you wake up. This will give the body a kick-start.
Invigorate the skin with a dry skin brush followed by a shower or bath. Massage the skin.
8.00am Time for breakfast. Try muesli made from sheep's milk yogurt, sunflower, sesame and pumpkin seeds with chopped dried apricots. Mix the seeds and apricots together and sprinkle over the top of a bowl of yogurt.
9.00am Give yourself a facial.
11.00am Time for relaxation and quality breathing.
1.00pm Lunch. Why not try a salad today and choose from the selection of recipes on pages 25-26? Finish with a piece of fruit. Make sure you eat your meal slowly and give your food time to digest before leaving the table.

2.00pm Relax for a while, read a book or watch the TV. Then go out for a brisk walk, starting off at a slow pace, then speeding up before gradually slowing down again. Plan your route so that it will take you at least 35 minutes to complete.

4.00pm Time for some pampering before you prepare the evening meal. Perhaps give yourself a foot massage – you might well need it after the walk. Place both hands flat on the tops of your feet, then brush them up towards your knees in long firm strokes. Repeat several times. Move your hands to the back of each leg in turn and press the flesh firmly, lifting it and pushing against the skin. Work the flesh back and forwards, taking care not to 'burn' it. Afterwards relax, listen to some music and drink a glass of fresh juice or a cup of herbal tea.

6.00pm Evening meal. Prepare a large plate of lightly steamed vegetables and season it with fresh herbs, nuts and seeds. Again, eat it slowly and be aware of each mouthful as you chew it. Remember, take time for it to digest.

7.00pm Visualization. Sit in a quiet room and focus all your thoughts on pleasing, positive images. Whenever random thoughts intervene, brush them aside and focus on the image in your mind's eye.

8.00pm Have a pleasant aromatherapy bath. Make sure the bathroom is warm and relaxing. Light the room with candles and play some of your favourite music. As you lie luxuriating in the warmth and listening to the music, begin taking deep breaths and, as you slowly exhale, feel the tensions ebbing away. After your bath, dry yourself, put on your nightwear and relax with a soothing cup of herbal tea.

Don't forget: As you complete each activity, tick it off on your chart. Before you go to sleep, remember to record in your diary how you felt, writing down both the good and the bad points.

Remainder of the week

For the remainder of week you should follow the same basic routine but choose some different foods, and experiment with different recipes. On day 3 exfoliate the skin and on day 5 take an Epsom salts bath. By day 6 you may start to feel a little bored, so make it more exciting by adding in extra little treats – have a manicure, give yourself a facial, watch a film one afternoon. Introducing subtle changes into the programme will help to maintain your interest.

End of the first week
- You will feel more alert
- Your skin will have taken on a better colour
- There may be spots on your back but these are the result of the toxins leaving your body
- You should feel fitter and look leaner because of the exercise

Measurements chart

The detox programme is not a weight-loss diet, but as you change your routine and reform your eating habits, you will find that you are not only looking good and feeling better, but you will have more energy and will have toned up those muscles too! You can record your measurements each week using this simple chart.

	Week 1	Week 2	Week 3	Week 4
Date				
Weight				
Bust				
Waist				
Hips				

Detox Days 8–14

You will have established a routine by now and perhaps made some changes to the overall schedule. So are you ready for week two?

7.00am Glass of hot water and lemon or lime juice. Skin brush, then a quick shower.

8.00am Breakfast – a large bowl of fresh fruit salad.

9.00am Have a facial sauna.

11.00am Visualization.

1.00pm Lunch – a nice, crunchy salad.

2.30pm Go for a swim. It will be time for some relaxation when you return home.

3.15pm Relaxation. Have a glass of herbal tea and an orange afterwards.

6.00pm Evening meal – stir-fried vegetables.

8.00pm Take an oatmeal bath (see box). Afterwards massage your feet with lots of moisturizer, then put on a pair of cotton socks. The perspiration from your feet will blend with the cream and leave your skin silky soft.

Don't forget: As you complete each activity, tick it off on your chart. Before you go to sleep, remember to write up your diary.

Remainder of the week

Keep up with the routine, even if you don't feel like it on some days. If you really feel down in the dumps, do something positive – go along to your local gym for a workout, and don't forget that a good dose of active housework is just as beneficial as a 35-minute swim in the pool. You may well be tempted to weigh yourself at this stage. If you have followed the programme correctly, you will probably have lost some weight.

Oatmeal bath

While the body is detoxing, the skin can sometimes become rather irritated. To alleviate this, try taking an oatmeal bath; it is very calming and soothing • Tie 450g (1lb) of uncooked oatmeal in an old nylon stocking and hang it under the hot water tap when running your bath • As the water flows through the oats, they will release their calming agents • Drop the oatmeal stocking into the water or use it as a sponge • Relax for about 20 minutes, long enough to allow the chemicals from the oats to infiltrate the skin • Then gently pat skin dry with a towel.

Changes that you should feel:

- Not so tired in the evening
- More alert and refreshed when you waken in the morning
- Your skin will look a lot better and any spots will probably have vanished
- You will be feeling much fitter and your body will look toned
- Your energy levels will be higher

Detox Days 15–21

You are now embarking on the second half of your detox programme. It probably hasn't been easy to get this far, but there is no turning back now.

Ỵou have come a long way and your body will be reaping the rewards of your endeavours.

7.00am Glass of hot water and lemon/lime juice. Skin brush, then a quick shower.
8.00am Breakfast – mix dried apricot seeds together and sprinkle them over the top of yogurt.
9.00am Give yourself a massage using some of your favourite aromatherapy essential oils.
11.00am Do some strenuous housework, vacuuming the carpets or washing the windows. The secret is to do it in half the time that you would normally take. So if a job usually takes you two hours, make sure that this time it only takes you one hour.
1.00pm Lunch – perhaps try some carrot soup.
2.00pm Visualization. At the end of the session, give yourself a facial sauna.
3.15pm Relaxation or try some yoga. Curl up with a book.
6.00pm Evening meal – you might choose some fish and a salad.
8.00pm Bath, then treat yourself to a manicure and pedicure.

Don't forget: As you complete each activity, tick it off on your chart. Before you go to sleep, remember to write up your diary.

Remainder of the week

Keep changing the foods you eat, the exercises you do and remember to keep including those little treats.

Changes that you should feel:
- Feeling totally refreshed and energetic
- Your skin should be smooth and unblemished with no dry patches
- You should have lost some weight
- Your body will feel and look much firmer
- The muscles at the tops of your arms and legs will be more defined
- You will feel on a high knowing that your body is now cleansed and working at its optimum level

Detox Days 22–28

Finally you are on the last lap. By now you have probably established a great routine of your own which may seem like second nature to you.

Now is not the time to give up or to falter. Keep going – only seven days to the finish!

7.00am Glass of hot water and lemon/lime juice. Skin brush, then a quick shower.
8.00am Breakfast – try a bowl of fresh fruit salad (you might want to prepare it the night before).
9.00am Breathing exercises. Give yourself a facial scrub.
11.00am Do some trampolining if you have one, or take yourself along to the local gym and enjoy a stimulating workout.
1.00pm Lunch – treat yourself to a tasty potato salad with fennel.
2.00pm Total relaxation.
3.15pm Visualization.
6.00pm Evening meal – a selection of roast vegetables might be nice.
8.00pm Take an Epsom salts bath.

The new you is revealed!
- Your skin will look better than it has for years
- Exercise will have become an integral part of your life
- Your body will look and feel in great shape
- You will feel on a total high – and so you should
- This is the healthiest you will have felt for years
Now is the time to weigh yourself and record your measurements in the chart on page 33. Look back at your original measurements to see how well you have done.

Activity Record Chart

Record your activities every day using this table

DAILY ACTIVITIES	1	2	3	4	5	6	7	8	9	10	11	12	13	14	15	16	17	18	19	20	21	22	23	24	25	26	27	28
Glass of hot water and lemon or lime juice																												
Shower/bath																												
Skin brushing																												
Moisturizing																												
Breakfast																												
Lunch																												
Dinner																												
1.75 litres (3 pints) water																												
Fruit																												
Goat's/sheep's milk																												
Goat's/sheep's cheese																												
Brown rice																												
Salad																												
Nuts																												
10 mins relaxation																												
5 mins breathing																												
5 mins visualization																												
Pampering																												
Exfoliate every three days																												
Laugh																												
Massage																												
Epsom salts bath 6 times during programme																												

Congratulations!

You've done it! You've successfully completed the 28-day detox programme. You will probably feel healthier than you have done for ages and you can be very proud of yourself.

Not only have you succeeded in cleansing your body of toxins, but in so doing you have emerged a fitter, happier and more confident person. But make sure, as you ride this wave of euphoria, that you don't slide back. You've come so far in the last 28 days that you don't want to risk losing all the hard-won gains.

Old habits are difficult to break, but during those dark moments when you felt that you couldn't continue, you didn't let those doubts undermine your determination. And now you have achieved this peak of good health, make sure that you hold on to it.

After all, you are the only person who can ensure that you do!

Try to make these recommendations part of your everyday life:
- Drink hot water and lemon/lime juice first thing in the morning
- Drink 1.75 litres (3 pints) of water every day
- Take the liver tonics daily – a snack of some black grapes plus a cup of fennel tea isn't hard to remember
- Take two kidney tonics each day – try adding a teaspoon of honey to your lemon juice and adding a cranberry supplement at breakfast time
- Eat three sensible meals a day

The 28 Day Plan

ENERGIZE

What Do We Mean By 'Energize'?

Does this sound familiar? Do you normally wake up in the mornings feeling just as tired as when you went to bed? Do you skip breakfast and then by mid-morning find yourself reaching for the biscuit tin?

Is lunch normally a quick sandwich and cup of coffee, only for you to find that by mid-afternoon your energy levels are dipping and so you need another biscuit and another cup of coffee? This describes a common but far from healthy lifestyle that could be draining your energy resources and preventing your body from working at its optimum.

If this reflects your life, this 28-day energize programme is just what you need. By the end of the four weeks you will look healthier, feel healthier and your batteries will be fully recharged.

What causes lack of energy?

There are many contributory factors that can lead to a feeling of lassitude and lack of energy. If you constantly feel tired and have checked with your doctor that there are no underlying medical conditions, perhaps it is time to consider other possible factors.

Bad diet

Fad dieting, erratic eating patterns, skipping meals or simply choosing a bad diet can play havoc with your overall well-being, draining your energy resources and leaving you feeling totally exhausted.

Persuade yourself never to skip a meal, especially breakfast first thing in the morning when the body is

Each day throughout your 28-day programme you should:
- Always eat breakfast
- Take one dose of aloe vera with your breakfast drink
- Eat three meals a day
- Take a multivitamin supplement for the first 15 days
- Drink at least 1.75 litres (3 pints) of water
- Eat at least three portions of fresh fruit
- Eat at least three portions of vegetables
- Eat one portion of a non-dairy product

at its lowest ebb and needs fuelling after a period of rest. Skipping meals during the day, surviving on cups of coffee and then eating a large meal in the evening, is very bad for you. Depriving the body of food during the day will deplete blood sugar levels and leave you feeling tired and even slightly light-headed. Your aim must be to eat three meals a day combined with low-fat healthy snacks in between if you feel peckish.

Stress

Whether it is caused by your job or the daily commitments of a busy housewife and mother, stress is an unavoidable fact of modern living. We all need a certain amount of stress in our lives in order to motivate us to do things, to get up in the morning or to pay the bills on time, but problems occur when stress works its way into the very fabric of your life and you end up with chronic physical and often emotional problems, including:

- Anxiety
- Depression
- Digestive problems
- Headaches
- Insomnia
- Irritable bowel syndrome
- Lack of energy

Stress isn't normally life-threatening but that doesn't mean that you should allow it to dominate your life. Learning to recognize and deal with stress is an invaluable lesson that you must learn. Coping with stress often involves doing something to take your mind off the immediate problem or situation – go out for a walk, listen to some music, do some housework, try anything that will distract your mind and help you to relax.

Whenever the body is experiencing stress, energy levels are sapped and several important nutrients, namely vitamins B and C and zinc, are used up. The only way to replenish that store is by eating foods containing high levels of these essential nutrients.

Vitamin B helps to maintain a healthy nervous system and release energy. It is found in potatoes, green vegetable, tomatoes, fresh and dried fruit, wheatgerm, wholegrain cereals, brown rice, eggs, dairy products, seafood, lean meat, liver, kidney, poultry, peas, beans, lentils, nuts and seeds.

Vitamin C helps the body to protect itself against possible infection. It is found in fresh fruits (particularly citrus fruit, i.e. oranges, grapefruit etc.), blackcurrants, fruit juices and fresh vegetables.

Zinc helps the body to resist possible infection. It is found in liver, red meat, egg yolks, dairy produce, wholegrain cereals, oysters and other shellfish.

Complex carbohydrates help to increase energy levels and relax the mind. They are found in bread, rice, pulses, oats, pasta and potatoes.

Alcohol

Most people enjoy the odd glass of wine or beer, but when alcohol becomes a prop to cope with an underlying problem, it takes on a very different aspect. Not only does alcohol act as a sedative, it also dehydrates you. That glass of wine drunk at lunchtime may well cause you to feel tired by mid-afternoon and one too many drinks taken at night may well cause restless sleep resulting in low energy levels the following morning.

The message is quite simple – take everything in moderation. One or two glasses of wine with a meal is fine; if you are going out for a couple of drinks in the evening, then make sure that you drink plenty of water before going to bed to prevent possible dehydration.

Sleep

We go to sleep in order to rest both the mind and body and to awaken fresh and invigorated the following morning. However, for some people bedtime is a nightmare because they spend most of the night

Alcohol

The British Medical Association recommends a weekly limit of 21 units of alcohol for men and 14 units for women, who are not pregnant, ideally spread over the full course of the week.

1 unit = $^{1}/_{2}$ pint of beer = a small glass of wine = a small glass of sherry = a small glass of spirits

lying awake staring into space. Sleeplessness or insomnia is a condition for which there are numerous treatments readily available, but before going to the doctor or chemist, why not try some self-help methods:

✓ Take some exercise during the day to keep the body active and to prepare it for rest at bedtime

✓ Try some relaxation methods to help you unwind

✓ Avoid drinking any stimulants, such as coffee or tea, preferably from early evening onwards

✓ Eat a healthy, balanced diet to encourage the body to function more effectively

✓ Take a good book to bed with you

Smoking

To maintain a high level of energy, the body requires a good supply of oxygen. Smoking reduces the amount of oxygen the body absorbs. Imagine every time you reach for a cigarette to give you an instant 'high', you are in fact doing the opposite. So give up smoking!

Signs of lack of energy:
- Inability to sleep
- Indigestion
- Irritability
- Lack of concentration
- Low blood sugar
- Mood swings
- Tiredness

Following the 28-day energize programme

The endless cycle of tiredness and feeling below par can become a daily way of life. But it needn't be that way. It is possible to free yourself from this routine and:

✓ Break the cycle of tiredness
✓ Enhance your brain power
✓ Help maintain stamina levels throughout the day
✓ Help you to find your natural, healthy body weight
✓ Leave you feeling invigorated and rejuvenated
✓ And put a spring back in your step!

Surprise friends, family, workmates (and more importantly yourself) by showing everyone how energetic and healthy you feel after following this 28-day programme.

To succeed on the programme:
- Adopt a positive attitude from the beginning
- Stay focused throughout
- Regard each new day as a new challenge
- Keep it exciting by adding different treatments from time to time
- Experiment with different foods
- And don't forget, pamper yourself

You are not advised to go on the energy programme if:
- You are pregnant or breastfeeding
- You are seeing your doctor for some medical condition
- You have anaemia
- You have Type 1 diabetes
- You are underweight
- You are experiencing extreme stress
- You are taking prescription medicines that cannot be discontinued

Food For Energy

An important lesson that you will learn while on this 28-day programme is how to recognize foods that are good for you and those that are not, those that improve your performance and those that impair it.

Once you can easily distinguish between the good foods from the bad foods, you will be able to eliminate the 'bad guys' from your diet and replace them with 'good guys'.

Energy is the driving force the body needs to:
✓ Enable muscles to move and carry out physical activities
✓ Maintain our normal body temperature
✓ Carry out essential physical functions, such as breathing, heartbeat and metabolism
✓ Promote tissue growth and repair

The body derives this energy from its intake of food. The main energy-producing nutrients are contained in three different food groups – carbohydrates, proteins and fats.

Carbohydrates

The main function of carbohydrates is to provide energy for the body. During digestion, carbohydrates are converted into glucose which is then absorbed into the bloodstream. The body uses the glucose for energy. If energy is not required immediately, it is stored in the muscles and the liver as glycogen where it remains available to be converted into glucose when extra energy is required.

Carbohydrate-rich foods:

- Baked beans
- Barley
- Brown rice
- Cereal
- Couscous
- Fresh fruit
- Grains
- Honey
- Juices
- Muesli
- Oat biscuits
- Pasta
- Pitta bread
- Porridge oats
- Potatoes
- Pulses
- Rice cakes
- Rice flour
- Rye bread
- Sweetcorn
- Tortillas
- Vegetables
- Wholemeal bread/rolls
- Wholemeal flour

Proteins

They are invaluable to the body principally for the role they play in repair and maintenance of the tissues, muscles and blood cells. An excess intake of protein is either converted into energy or converted into fat and stored in the body for emergency use.

Protein-rich foods:

- Brown bread
- Butter
- Chicken
- Chickpeas, lentils
- Cooking oils
- Dairy products, i.e. milk, cheese, yogurt, goat's milk cheese
- Fish – fresh, frozen, canned
- Kidney
- Liver
- Meat – bacon, beef, lamb, pork
- Meat products – beefburgers, sausages
- Nuts
- Quorn – meat substitute
- Soya
- Turkey

Fats

The role fats play in the body's energy budget is to supply it with a concentrated source of energy and also fatty acids vital for the maintenance of a healthy skin and the regulation of body functions.

Fat-rich foods: these should be eaten sparingly

- Cakes
- Puddings
- Ice cream
- Crisps
- Sweeteners

If you have a sweet tooth, then avoid sugar and artificial sweeteners, instead try healthier alternatives:

- Blackstrap molasses
- Honey
- Fructose powder (fruit sugar)
- Real maple syrup

Foods that are good and bad for maintaining energy levels

Bad guys:	Good guys:
Sugary cereals	Porridge, muesli
Pasties, pies, sausages	Fish, poultry, lamb
Biscuits, chocolate	Bananas, dried fruit
Chips	Baked potatoes
Salted nuts, crisps	Sesame seeds, fresh nuts
White bread	Wholemeal, brown bread
Sweet fizzy drinks	Fresh juice, water
Cooking oil	Extra virgin olive oil
Margarine	Butter/non-hydrogenated margarine
Packaged orange juice	Home-made apple/grape juice
Coffee, tea	Water, freshly squeezed fruit or vegetable juice, herbal tea
Dairy milk	Soya milk
Cow's milk cheese	Sheep's or goat's milk cheese
Beef or pork	Lean lamb, lamb's liver

Maintaining energy levels

Most people enjoy the instant buzz you get after eating a bar of chocolate or drinking a cup of coffee. You instantly feel re-energized both physically and mentally. Yet those feelings are short-lived because once the initial 'lift' has waned, energy levels plummet.

However, on the other side of the equation from those foods that can drain energy levels, there are other foods that can keep energy levels evenly balanced. Here is a list showing you some examples of the 'bad guys' – those foods that give you an instant, but short-lived, energy boost – while on the opposite side are the 'good guys', the healthier energy-boosting alternatives.

Write them out on a piece of paper and stick it up on your kitchen wall, so that you can refer to the list throughout your programme.

Eating for energy

While on the 28-day programme your main aim is to eat for energy so:

• Always eat breakfast
• Reduce, or better still cut out, stimulants such as coffee, chocolate or sugar
• Do not go for long periods through the day without eating something
• Eating small meals little and often puts less strain on the digestive system and burns calories far more efficiently
• If you find that your energy levels are low, increase the protein content of your diet. Often protein foods will satisfy the appetite for longer than carbohydrates

What to buy

Shopping for food can be a nightmare, especially if you are trying to keep a mental note of those foods that will provide extra energy and those that are depriving your body of energy, however tempting they may look.

Here are some guidelines to make that choice a little easier.

Fresh fruit

Fruit provides most of our daily intake of vitamin C. Aim to eat two or three pieces of fresh fruit each day.

• Apples
• Apricots
• Bananas
• Blackberries
• Blackcurrants
• Blueberries
• Cherries
• Dried figs
• Grapefruit
• Grapes
• Figs
• Kiwi fruit
• Lemons
• Limes
• Mangos
• Melons
• Nectarines
• Papaya
• Passionfruit
• Peaches
• Pears
• Pineapple
• Raisins
• Raspberries
• Strawberries
• Sultanas

Vegetables

Vegetables are good foods. They are packed with essential fibre, vitamins and minerals. Aim to include at least two or three portions each day.

• Artichokes
• Asparagus
• Aubergines
• Avocados
• Bamboo shoots
• Beansprouts
• Beetroot
• Broccoli
• Brussels sprouts
• Cabbage (dark green is healthier)
• Calabrese
• Capsicums
• Carrots
• Cauliflower
• Celeriac
• Chicory
• Chives
• Courgettes
• Endive
• Garlic
• Kale
• Leeks
• Lettuce (dark green is healthier)
• Mangetout
• Marrows
• Mushrooms
• Mustard and cress
• Onions (spring onions too)
• Shallots
• Spinach
• Swedes
• Tomatoes
• Turnips
• Watercress

The 'try to avoid at all times' foods

If at all possible, avoid the following foods which may give you an instant high, but then several hours later you will feel the lows.

• Beef (unless organic)
• Chocolate
• Cheese – coloured, smoked, processed
• Cow's milk – drink sparingly
• Diet drinks
• Diet foods
• Fizzy drinks
• Hydrogenated oils
• Ice-cream
• Low-fat foods with lots of additives
• Margarine spreads
• Peanuts
• Pork (unless organic)
• Refined white flour
• Salty foods
• Sugar
• Sugar-coated cereals
• Wheat-based breakfast foods

Supplements

This 28-day energize programme is not a diet; there is no calorie counting involved, just sensible healthy eating combined with a disciplined exercise programme. At the beginning of the programme you may well benefit from including a daily multivitamin supplement. Experts are convinced that supplements are invaluable for providing the essential support our bodies need to cope with the energy-draining effects of modern day life.

Certain vitamins and minerals are essential for helping the body to produce energy. Many of them can be found in the 'good guys' food list.

Aloe vera

A daily dose of aloe vera is used as a digestive tonic and is reputed to raise energy levels and enhance well-being. Take it daily mixed with fruit juice as a pre-breakfast drink.

Fast foods

Convenient and quick, the perfect standby, we seem to have become a generation of convenience food eaters, whether it is a beefburger dripping with tomato ketchup, a plate of fish and chips swimming in salt and vinegar, or a frozen ready-made meal packed with additives and preservatives.

The occasional takeaway or frozen meal is fine, but a diet based mainly on such foods is badly deficient in a number of essential nutrients. The dishes are also high in calories, sodium and fat.

If you really can't cope without a burger, then limit yourself to one as a special treat at the weekend and even then try to choose healthier options:

✓ Ask for small plain burgers, instead of big ones
✓ Miss out on the melted cheese, mayonnaise and other selected toppings
✓ Have a plain glass of milk instead of a milkshake
✓ Instead of chips, order a side salad

Nutrient	Role	Food sources
Iron	Needed for manufacturing red blood cells	Red meat, sardines, egg yolk, leafy vegetables
Zinc	Essential for maintaining a healthy immune system	Grains, nuts, fish, red meat, peanuts
Magnesium	Essential for building healthy bones	Green vegetables, wholegrain cereals, nuts
B vitamins	Essential for releasing energy from food	Broccoli, nuts, yeast, wholemeal bread
Vitamin C	Essential for healthy gums, teeth, skin, bones etc	Oranges, kiwi fruit, tomatoes
Vitamin E	Weakens unstable substances that can cause damage to cells	Green vegetables, nuts, vegetable oils

Drinking For Energy

Do you recognize this scenario? Get up in the morning, grab a cup of coffee before dashing off to work or getting the children ready for school. Mid-morning, feeling tired, time for another cup or two of coffee. Lunchtime, no time for lunch so grab another cup of coffee and a chocolate biscuit...

If you can identify with this pattern of behaviour, then you are by no means alone. Probably 80 per cent of the population crawl out of bed in the morning, gulp down a cup of coffee before dashing off to work or getting the children off to school, only to find that by mid-morning they are 'dead on their feet' and in desperate need of something to keep them going. One cup of coffee can seem the perfect pick-me-up, but if you drink more than six cups a day, you are spiralling into caffeine dependency, so perhaps it is time to consider gradually weaning yourself off the stuff and replacing it with herbal tea.

What to drink

Maintaining a healthy balance of fluid in the body is important, provided that it is the right type of fluid. Experts recommend that we should aim to drink at least 1.75 litres (3 pints) of water a day to help clean out toxins and keep our bodies in tip-top condition.

A glass of hot water with a squeeze of lemon or lime added to it taken first thing in the morning is ideal for refreshing the mouth and kick-starting the body into action. But some people tend to prefer a glass of a sweet fizzy drink, or a cup of black coffee – neither of which is healthy and neither of which will sustain energy levels.

Although we say that everything can be taken in moderation while on the 28-day energize programme, there are some drinks that should definitely be avoided or at least limited.

Good	Bad
Fresh juice	Alcohol
Fresh vegetable juice	Coffee
Herbal tea	Sweet fizzy drinks
Low-calorie drinks	
Milk	
Water	

Fact A 330ml (11½ fl oz) can of non-diet cola drink contains over seven teaspoons of sugar!

Fact The caffeine in coffee stimulates the brain and keeps you awake, but a high regular intake, i.e. more than eight cups a day, may well increase the risk of osteoporosis in later life. It causes migraine in those susceptible to it and can also be addictive.

Fact Drinking excessive amounts of alcohol destroys important vitamins A, C and E that are needed for general health and also stamina.

Sports drinks

It may be tempting to buy commercial 'isotonic' sports drinks that contain levels of salts and sugars for energy. A less expensive, and just as effective, alternative is to dilute fruit juice 1:1 with water.

Making your own energy drinks

Fresh is best, even when it comes to drinks, so why spend money on buying expensive pre-packaged 'fresh juice' when you can make it at home for less than half the cost and with the added knowledge that you know that what the drink contains is only the best!

Both fresh fruit and vegetables are bursting with so much natural goodness that the benefits of consuming them are fundamental to good health. Once you begin drinking them, you will physically feel much healthier, your skin will become clearer, your eyes will sparkle and your hair shine. After all, what better way is there of ensuring that the body gets all the vitamins, minerals and enzymes it needs in a form that is readily absorbed into the body? And so even if you don't fancy eating any fruit or vegetables on some days, you can still make sure you have your daily quota by drinking it out of a glass.

Anytime of the day drinks

Appetising apple Chop up two medium-sized apples and pop them into a juicer. There is no need to remove the core or seeds.

Strawberry juice Take a punnet of strawberries, wash and then pluck off the green stalks before putting the strawberries into the juicer whole. Blend them to make a delicious summer drink.

Energy cocktail

1 banana
1 mango
1 teaspoon honey
Half a medium-sized pineapple

Make your own special cocktail for when your energy levels are flagging – simply pop all the ingredients into a blender and whizz them together. Within minutes you will have a deliciously tasty drink.

Red as a beetroot

If you fancy your quota of vegetables in a glass, then beetroot, which is packed with vitamins and minerals, makes a strong and tasty drink, especially when cucumber is added.

110g (4oz) raw beetroot
280g (10oz) cucumber or half a large one

Wash any soil from the beetroot. Remove any hairy roots, then slice and pop the pieces into the juicer. Do not peel the cucumber, simply rinse the skin in water. Slice it into pieces and place it together with the beetroot in the juicer.

Pep up

4 oranges
1 lemon
1 teaspoon honey
Ice cubes

Mix the juice of the oranges and lemon into a tumbler, adding one teaspoon of honey. Serve with ice for a wonderfully energizing and refreshing drink packed with vitamin C.

Banana whizz

2 bananas, chopped
4 oranges
1 pot of low-fat natural yogurt

Into a blender add the two chopped bananas, the flesh of four oranges and the pot of yogurt. Blend until it turns into a purée and then serve.

Energy Recipes

The great thing about the Energize programme is that you can eat a wide variety of
healthy foods that will make you feel good and maintain your energy levels throughout
the day. You will be amazed at the difference changing your daily diet will make
to your overall sense of well-being.

Remember, you don't have to eat huge meals –
small frequent snacks throughout the day are
often better in helping to maintain a constant energy
supply and to avoid fatigue setting in. Nutritionists
recommend that you aim to consume 50 per cent of
your daily calories in the form of carbohydrates,
10-15 per cent in the form of proteins and 35 per
cent in the form of fats.

Breakfast recipes

The longest gap between any of the daily meals is the
period between dinner and breakfast the following
morning. During the eight or so hours that you are
sleeping, the body is still actively working, repairing
cells and keeping the heart and organs functioning,
and it derives energy from the store of sugar or
glucose held in the blood, liver and muscles. It is small
wonder that by sunrise, and with more than half of
the body's glucose used up, it needs refuelling. This
emphasizes the importance of a good breakfast.

If you skip breakfast just to enjoy another 20
minutes' lie-in, the chances are that you will function
perfectly well for the first few hours of the day, but
once your blood sugar levels drop, poor concentration,
lethargy and irritability will set in and by mid-morning
you will probably be eating your third chocolate
biscuit or drinking your fifth cup of coffee.

From now on, things are going to change! Make a
determined effort every day to have a good breakfast,
prepare it the night before if that's easier.

Breakfast choices Stay clear of foods that are high in
sugar, such as doughnuts or sugary cereals. Although
they provide a quick energy buzz, this will leave you
feeling tired a few hours later.

The ideal breakfast foods contain a combination of
carbohydrate, fibre and protein, each helping to

stabilize blood sugar levels. Try these suggestions:
• Chopped apple with unsweetened yogurt and ground sesame seeds sprinkled over the top
• Scrambled eggs with rye toast
• Mix a chopped banana and a small pot of low-fat yogurt with some unsweetened muesli
• Yogurt with wheatgerm, honey and stewed dried apricots on top
• Toasted bagel with cottage cheese
• A muffin topped with a little fat-free cheese and grilled until brown. Serve with a glass of freshly squeezed orange juice
• A generous serving of high-fibre cereal. Topped with fruit, such as raisins or raspberries, with fat-free milk for a perfect, nutritious, quick breakfast.

Never skip breakfast
• It is the most important meal of the day and helps to refuel the body after it has rested
• It will discourage you from grabbing a sugary snack mid-morning
• It will help to maintain your sugar levels
• Research studies have found that adults who eat a balanced breakfast sustain better mental performance throughout the day

Liquid breakfast
Many people baulk at the idea of eating any solid food in the morning, but there are lots of healthy liquid alternatives.

Drink up
If you generally start the day with coffee or tea, why not try something more uplifting that will not leave you feeling sluggish by mid-morning? Herbal and fruit teas not only have their own individual tastes but many beneficial health properties too:

Camomile: Long used to help ease digestive problems and calm the nerves. Also said to aid sleep.

Lemon Balm: Relieves tension without causing sleepiness; helps digestion.

Limeflower: Eases stress headaches and also aid sleep.

Rosemary: If you need a pick-me-up for those early mornings, this is the tea to drink as it is known to increase alertness and give energy levels a boost.

Thyme: To lift your spirits, try a cup of thyme.

Morning lift
150ml (5fl oz) skimmed milk
1 teaspoon clear honey
1 banana, chopped
150ml (5fl oz) natural yogurt
100g (3^1/$_2$oz) frozen berry fruits (whatever are in season)

Mix all the ingredients together in a blender for a high-protein breakfast drink that will keep your energy levels surging.

Bouncing banana
1 banana, chopped
2 teaspoons lemon juice
1 tablespoon fine oatmeal
2 teaspoons clear honey
3 tablespoons natural yogurt
150ml (5fl oz) semi-skimmed milk

Blend all the ingredients together until smooth.

Lunchtime ideas

Eating a good energy-based lunch can see you through quite happily until your evening meal with no horrendous 'lows' on the way. But you must choose energy-based foods. Here are some ideas:

Jacket potato Once regarded as one of the 'bad guys', potatoes have in fact been promoted to the 'good guys' list, because it isn't the vegetable that does the damage but rather how it is prepared. A potato is a high-carbohydrate food that contains protein, fibre and vitamin C as well as other essential nutrients, and so it is the ideal lunchtime food. One of the best ways to eat it is in its jacket.

Wash one large potato thoroughly and stab it evenly with a skewer before popping into the microwave (check your microwave instructions for recommended cooking times) or put it into the oven (200°C/400°F/gas mark 6) for about 90 minutes.

For some nutritious fillings try:

- 50g (2oz) prawns combined with 50g (2oz) sweetcorn, 1 tablespoon salad dressing and 1 tablespoon tomato ketchup
- 50g (2oz) cooked chicken blended with 1 tablespoon low fat natural yogurt, diced red and green peppers and 1 tablespoon salad dressing
- 110g (4oz) can baked beans with ¼ teaspoon chilli powder
- 200g (7oz) small can spaghetti hoops and 2 tomatoes
- Chopped mushrooms fried in a little extra virgin olive oil
- Put 100g (4oz) low-fat cottage cheese, 2 tablespoons low-fat yogurt, 1 teaspoon garlic purée and 1 teaspoon dried herbs in a bowl and mix well.

Home-made coleslaw

This recipe makes sufficient for four servings, so store some in the refrigerator for the next day.

1 carrot
3 salad onions
2 red radishes
Stick of celery
Chunk of crisp lettuce
1 pepper (red, green or yellow)
Soy sauce
1 tablespoon cider vinegar
Herb salt (available from healthfood shops)
Black pepper

Wash, peel and grate the vegetables until they are finely shredded. Add in a shake of soy sauce, the cider vinegar, and a sprinkling of salt and pepper. Mix thoroughly. Once the jacket potato is cooked, slice it through the centre and pack in a portion of the coleslaw. It's healthy, nutritious and satisfying!

Super sandwiches

Often a sandwich is more appealing at lunchtime than a full meal and can be more convenient, as most cafés, supermarkets and corner shops sell them. But although it is easier to buy pre-packaged sandwiches than to make your own, there is always a concern about the ingredients used. So, whenever possible, prepare your own, preferably the night before so there are no excuses the following morning that you haven't time to do it. If they are wrapped in foil, they will keep fresh in the refrigerator overnight.

Here are some tasty lunchtime suggestions

• 2 slices of wholemeal bread with tuna and lettuce. Plus an apple.
• Pitta bread filled with baked beans
• Pitta bread with avocado and tomato

Alternatively, try some of these ideas for something a little bit different.

Banana surprise Mash up a banana adding a squeeze of lemon juice. Add crispy bits of bacon and put the mixture between two slices of wholemeal bread.

Fishy treat Drain a can of sardines or mackerel and mash the fish. Put the mix between two slices of wholemeal bread along with several slices of tomato and some lettuce.

Chicken parcel Perfect if you had chicken for dinner the evening before and still have some cold leftovers. Chop up the chicken and mix it with some low-fat natural yogurt with a few chopped spring onions. Place crispy lettuce on two slices of wholemeal bread and spoon the mixture over the top.

Pitta celebration Take 1 pitta bread, ¹/2 ripe avocado, 1 chopped spring onion, 2 lettuce leaves, 2 tablespoons alfalfa sprouts, 1 sliced tomato, 1 teaspoon vinaigrette dressing, cayenne pepper and lemon juice. Mash the avocado and spring onions in a

bowl. Pour in the vinaigrette dressing and add a pinch of cayenne pepper. When thoroughly blended, spoon the mixture into the pitta bread, finishing off with the lettuce leaves, alfalfa sprouts and tomato. Serve with a squeeze of lemon juice and a pinch of cayenne.

Vegetable surprise

A perfect light lunch on its own or equally as tasty if served to accompany a larger meal.

Small head broccoli

2 carrots

1 leek

1 courgette

Soy sauce

110g (4oz) mozzarella cheese, sliced

Wash the vegetables thoroughly and chop them into small chunks (you can include the broccoli stalks if they are tender). Steam the vegetables until just cooked. Drain well and transfer to a shallow ovenproof dish. Sprinkle over a few drops of soy sauce. Spread the cheese over the top and pop the dish under the grill until the cheese is golden brown.

Dinnertime recipes

Tasty burgers

225g (8oz) cooked chicken, minced
50g (2oz) onion, grated
275g (10oz) cottage cheese
1 teaspoon mixed herbs
Salt and black pepper

Mix the chicken and grated onion together in a bowl, then season with salt and pepper. Add the cottage cheese and mixed herbs and stir thoroughly. Shape the mixture into four round burgers and place them on a plate in the refrigerator for 1-2 hours. When you are ready to cook, place the burgers under a hot grill for approximately 5 minutes for each side. When the burgers are a golden colour, serve them with a fresh mixed salad.

Curry in a hurry

This recipe will serve four.
85g (3oz) soya chunks (weight when dry)
400g (14oz) can tomatoes
1 medium apple, chopped
2 teaspoons pickle
1 teaspoon tomato purée
1 medium onion, chopped
1 bay leaf
1 tablespoon curry powder

Add 2 cups of boiling water to a basin and soak the soya chunks for approximately 10 minutes. Place all the ingredients, together with the soya, in a saucepan and bring to the boil. Cover the saucepan and leave to simmer for 1 hour, occasionally stirring. If the mixture appears slightly thin, remove the lid and increase the heat slightly until the sauce begins to thicken. Serve with brown rice.

Egg fried rice

1 small onion
1 large mushroom
1 tablespoon virgin olive oil
$^1/_4$ teaspoon paprika
$^1/_4$ teaspoon curry powder
1 tablespoon dried herbs
2 large eggs, hard boiled and chopped
Half small red pepper
100g (4oz) boiled brown rice
50g (2oz) cooked petit pois
Soy sauce
Lettuce

Slice the onion and the mushroom and fry in olive oil for 2 minutes. Add the curry powder, paprika and dried herbs and stir. Shell the eggs and cut into small pieces. Wash and de-seed the red pepper and then chop into small pieces. Add the pepper, rice, peas and soy sauce and heat thoroughly. Before serving, mix in the chopped egg and transfer onto a bed of lettuce.

Delicious desserts

Sweets don't always have to be packed with calories, they can be healthy and great energy boosters. These treats are great for times when you are in a hurry.

Grape salad Scoop out the flesh from half a melon into a dessert dish or tall sundae glass. Take a handful of seedless grapes and cut them in half. Pile them on top of the melon and garnish with sprigs of mint.

Melon shocker Scoop out the flesh from half a melon and put it into a bowl. Add a carton of natural yogurt, stir and chill before serving.

The whole family will love these delicious desserts. Each recipe serves four.

Mandarin jelly

300g (11 oz) can mandarins in natural juice
450ml (15fl oz) unsweetened orange juice
1 sachet powdered gelatine

Drain the juice from the mandarins and mix with the orange juice. Pour half the liquid into a bowl and sprinkle on the gelatine. Stir well and transfer to a saucepan. Warm gently over a low heat until all the gelatine has dissolved. Add the remaining fruit juice slowly, stirring continuously. Remove from the heat and pour into a bowl. Leave to cool for two minutes before adding the mandarin pieces which will sink to the bottom of the bowl. Cover the bowl and place in the refrigerator until set.

If you feel peckish during the day, eat:
- An orange
- A banana
- Handful of grapes
- Handful of cherries
- Dried fruit
- A carrot
- An apple
- Low-fat yogurt

Pineapple delight

14oz can of crushed pineapple in natural juice
1 packet sugar-free lemon jelly to make 600ml (1 pint)
150ml (5fl oz) carton low-fat yogurt

Drain the pineapple and reserve the juice. Follow the instructions to make up the jelly, using the pineapple juice and making the quantity of liquid up to 600ml (1 pint). Stir in the crushed pineapple and place in the refrigerator until set. Now for the fun part – once the jelly is firm, use a fork to break it up and then mix in the yogurt. Great on its own or with fresh fruit.

Raise Your Energy

To achieve the ultimate success on the Energize programme, which is to feel rejuvenated and invigorated, it is important that you include each of the following elements in your 28-day plan...

Energy shower

There is nothing like an early morning energy shower to kick-start the body into action, so first thing each morning jump into the shower and, if you feel brave enough, when you are about ready to come out, turn the cold tap full on for a few minutes.

After showering, invigorate your body and boost circulation by slapping yourself all over. Using the flats of your hands and slap from toes to hip, wrist to shoulder and all over your chest, shoulders and torso before rubbing dry with a towel.

Make sure that each day you:
- Take a daily energy shower
- Do some stretching and flexing of the body at the start of each day
- Spend 30 minutes exercising
- Spend 20 minutes in 'hibernation'
- Spend 5 minutes practising quality breathing
- Spend 10 minutes hypnotizing yourself
- Each day pamper yourself in some way
- Laugh heartily each day
- Aim to get a good night's sleep

Stretch

A good stretch a day makes aches go away. Try it for yourself. Perform each movement slowly.
1. Link your fingers and raise them above your head until you feel the whole of your upper body stretch.
2. Still keeping your fingers linked, stretch your arms out in front at the same time stretching your back.
3. Place your arms behind you, still with your fingers linked, and as you stretch feel the pull across your chest.
4. Drop your left ear down to your left shoulder, stretching out the muscles of the neck and shoulders, then do the same on the other side.
5. To stretch the back of your neck, drop your chin down to your chest.

Exercise

Exercise to energize. Keep those three words firmly focused in your mind's eye – write them in large print on a piece of paper and pin it up in the kitchen or bathroom so that whenever you feel sluggish, you can remind yourself and keep yourself motivated.

If, apart from walking to the shops, you haven't exercised since the day you left school, then you are bound to feel a little apprehensive. But all the experts advocate a daily dose of physical activity to help us stay emotionally and physically fit. Exercise actually increases energy levels by releasing endorphins which are the body's natural 'high' hormones that make you feel great.

Exercising has many other positive benefits:

✓ It gives you greater stamina

✓ It improves posture

✓ It can help you to relax and sleep better

✓ It helps you to deal with everyday stresses more effectively

If you have not exercised for a long while, take it easy at first. Don't overdo it – begin your regime gradually, building up day by day until at the end of the programme exercising will have become part of your daily routine.

On the first day or so, just do some gentle exercise, walking to the shops instead of taking the car or getting the bus. Go for a swim or perhaps enrol for a class at your local gym. As your stamina and confidence grow, then you can increase the amount of exercise you take until you actually begin to feel physically tired. The key advice is to participate in activities that you enjoy three times a week, but never to exhaust yourself. If you are stuck for ideas, try some of these:

Jogging, tennis, cycling, skipping. These sports are ideal for raising the heartbeat and should ideally be done for 20 minutes three times a week for a safe energy-building programme.

Bouncing. Jogging and jumping on a trampoline is great aerobic exercise. It raises the heartbeat and increases lung capacity without putting unnecessary pressure on knee joints. You could join the local gym or invest in a mini-trampoline to use at home, indoors or out in the garden on days when the weather is good. All the family will be keen to use it!

Walking, swimming, spring-cleaning or digging the garden. These are all forms of exercise that are good for the body. Whatever activity you choose, the most important thing is to do it regularly in order for it to be fully effective. Like most things in life, you only get out what you put in.

Health check

- Before taking up any sport, check with your doctor if you are pregnant or have a medical condition
- Always warm up before starting the routine and cool down slowly after
- Never increase the intensity or length spent exercising if you feel any physical discomfort
- Make sure that you drink plenty of fluids while exercising

Fact Scientists have discovered that the ideal time of the day to work out is between 4pm and 7pm. According to research, by late afternoon our body temperature, muscle flexibility and strength have all reached their peak levels.

Restoring Energy

It is amazing how a daily 20-minute mini-break can restore depleted energy resources and recharge flagging batteries.

Hibernation

Simply find a place where you feel totally relaxed and for 20 minutes allow yourself to switch off.

Think about no-one and nothing. Lie down and listen to some favourite music, take a candlelit bath, or even close your eyes and imagine you are a castaway on a desert island with the man of your dreams, and enjoy your 20-minute fantasy!

Deep breathing

There is nothing quite so refreshing or relaxing as five minutes of deep, steady breathing to blow away those cobwebs. And deep breathing is also excellent for helping you to de-stress.

1. Sit in a quiet room.
2. If you are wearing a skirt or trousers, undo the waistband so there is ample space for you to expand your tummy.
3. Close your eyes, now slowly breathe in through your nose, holding that breath for a count of five, and then, to a count of five, slowly exhale through your mouth.
4. Repeat this again several times.

Self-hypnotism to combat stress

It is a well-known fact that the growing pressures of everyday modern life have made stress one of the biggest health problems of the age. But on this 28-day programme you will learn how to deal with stress; whenever you find yourself in a stressful situation, you will be able to cope if you follow this simple nine-point plan.

1. Make sure that you are alone in the room. Sit down and close your eyes.
2. Say to yourself, 'I am going to overcome this tiredness'.
3. Now imagine a still river with clear crystal water that tempts you to dive in headfirst.
4. Think of yourself diving into that river and, as you do so, become aware of your tiredness gradually drifting away into the distance like ripples spreading across the surface of the water and getting further and further away.
5. When you can no longer see the ripples, breathe in deeply allowing yourself to float totally free and relaxed.

6. Begin stretching your body. Feel every part being stretched gently to its limit, focus your mind's eye on this image.

7. Now imagine that you are sinking deeper and deeper. Allow your body to luxuriate in the sensation of the water as it laps gently around you.

8. Rise up to the surface and bring yourself back to the real world.

9. Breathe out and then breathe in, become conscious of your lungs being filled to their full capacity with air. As you breathe out slowly, be aware that every last bit of stale air is being squeezed out of your lungs. Then open both eyes.

Whenever you feel totally stressed, this is your own secret Shangri-La. It will take several attempts to feel the benefits, but the more your practise, the easier it will become and the more totally relaxed your body will feel.

Laughter

Can you remember the last time you had a jolly good laugh or was it so long ago, you've forgotten? Experts have found that people who use humour to cope with stress experience:

✓ Less tension
✓ Less fatigue
✓ Less anger
✓ Less depression

And, furthermore, laughing:

✓ Relaxes face muscles
✓ Exercises internal muscles
✓ Deepens breathing
✓ Improves blood circulation
✓ Lowers blood pressure and releases endorphins, the feel-good chemicals that are the body's natural painkillers

Or hire a comedy video, read a funny book or watch your favourite TV sitcom and have a really good laugh.

Sleep

We need sleep almost as much as we need food to fuel our bodies. Without sleep and rest, the body cannot function at its optimum level; it is deprived of the invaluable time it needs to repair cells and recuperate from the rigours of the day. Yet for thousands of people night time is literally a nightmare, a period when they lie awake until the early hours of the morning staring into space. Others spend the entire night tossing and turning in bed and when daylight comes, they are too tired to get up.

Insomnia is a medical condition and there are many medicines and treatments available to help sufferers. However, before going to your doctor, why not try some of these self-help methods?

1. Sleep with the window slightly open.

2. Make sure that the mattress is firm and supportive and that you have sufficient pillows.

3. Eat at least five hours before going to bed.

4. Try and go to bed at the same time every evening.

5. Make sure that you do some exercise during the day. This helps to keep the mind and body active and so ready for rest at night time.

6. Try some relaxation exercises before bedtime.

7. Eat a healthy balanced diet to help your body function more effectively.

Pamper yourself

And why not? You deserve it, you're a good person! Go out and treat yourself to the biggest, brightest bunch of flowers that you can find and if people ask whom they are for, tell them 'They're for me, because I deserve them'.

Maintaining The Programme

There will be times during the 28-day Energize programme when you will feel like giving it all up, but such negative thoughts are only to be expected: ignore them. After all, they are only thoughts.

Consider adding some extra treats into your programme to provide little rewards to keep yourself motivated. For instance, give yourself a face mask, or how about a foot mask, or pampering yourself with a luxury bath? It's important to keep your spirits up throughout the programme. If you get low moments of despondency when you feel exhausted from your daily exercise routine, just remember exercise to energize.

Face mask

Do you ever feel as if your skin could do with some tightening up and that you would love a face mask, but you cannot afford one? Then try this home-made mask which is suitable for all skin types and really does tighten the skin, albeit temporarily.

1. You need one egg and one tablespoon of honey.
2. Separate the egg and beat the white until it is stiff.
3. Add the honey and stir thoroughly.
4. Apply the mixture all over the face and leave it in place for 20 minutes.
5. Rinse it off using warm water.

If you have particularly dry skin, add several drops of peach kernel oil as a moisturizer.

Foot mask

Your feet are bound to take a lot of punishment once you begin exercising. To keep them in tip-top condition and to prevent the skin from drying out, pamper them with a refreshing foot mask.

1. You need two bananas, two teaspoons of olive oil, two tablespoons of fine sea salt and the juice of half a lemon.
2. Mash the bananas up in a bowl into which you should then tip the rest of the ingredients.
3. Mix everything thoroughly, rest your feet on a towel and then massage the mixture into them.
4. Leave it on for approximately ten minutes and then wash it off using warm water.

Afterwards, apply lots of moisturizer to your feet.

Luxury bath

You will find that there is nothing quite as therapeutic as a luxury bath simply because the essential oils added to the bathwater immediately release calming aromas. Simply add five drops of marjoram and ten drops of lavender oil to a hot bath. Switch off the lights and soak in the bath for a luxurious 20 minutes at least.

Colour me happy

Does wearing a bright red T-shirt make you feel happy or sad? Or do you feel calm when wearing a green sweater? According to scientists, colours can have a strong effect upon our emotions, and so bringing colour into one's life can really help to lift the spirits and alleviate feelings of lethargy.

When energy levels are low, you inevitably feel a little downhearted and nothing seems to feel or look right on you. So when, halfway through the programme, you find you begin to feel in need of cheering up, treat yourself to a new T-shirt, some pretty flowers or even a new lamp to brighten up your living room or bedroom!

Certain colours can influence your feelings:
Blue: Invokes a feeling of calm.
Green: A soothing colour, one that is said to alleviate feelings of anxiety or fear.
Orange: Enhances enthusiasm, creativity and courage.
Red: Gives of a sense of warmth and excitement.
Violet: Improves self-confidence and encourages intuitive thinking.
Yellow: Promotes hope, happiness and consideration.

Think positive

You may well face days during the programme when you feel down, but hidden beneath those feelings are positive emotions lying in wait. Every day, try to work hard to bring them to the surface. When you feel good about yourself, you can begin to understand the type of person you are and accept your characteristics, even your imperfections. Experts have found that people who are positive and optimistic usually enjoy long-term good health.

How to lift negative emotions

• Keep a diary of those negative thoughts, write them down at the end of the day and then start to challenge them by putting positive messages alongside. 'I don't feel that I am any more energetic' might be the negative message, 'but you are doing a lot more than before' could be a positive reply.

• If you have times when you feel anxious or stressed out, stop and think about happy occasions and try to remember how they felt.

• Ignore negative thoughts whenever they worm their way into your mind. After all, millions of thoughts pass through our minds each day; thoughts can't harm you.

• Why not set yourself a challenge while on the programme – take up a new sport and aspire to a certain level of proficiency. By achieving this, you will feel much more confident of your abilities.

Energize: Days 1–7

You've done all the preparatory work and now can look forward to the 28-day Energize programme. By the end it you should feel invigorated and rejuvenated. Whether you are a working woman or a busy mother at home, the next 28 days should witness some of the biggest changes that you will ever make to your life...so be prepared!

Draw up a chart (see page 67) and stick it on your fridge or kitchen wall so that you will remember exactly what you must include on each day of your 28 day programme.

Keep a diary and record in it all the day's activities, what you ate, how you felt when you woke up, how you relaxed. At the end of each day summarize how you feel. Naturally on some days you will find more to write about than on others, but it will help to keep you motivated if you keep this diary and refer to it for encouragement when you have down days. Weigh yourself today only!

Here is a typical plan for day 1, but of course times and the order in which activities are done may differ, according to your individual lifestyle and work commitments.

6.45am Aim to get up 20 minutes earlier than normal. Kick-start the body by drinking a glass of hot water with a squeeze of lemon added to it.

7.15am Spend ten minutes stretching and flexing the whole body.

8.00am Take an energy shower or bath, slapping the skin before towelling yourself dry.

8.45am Time for breakfast. Have some wheatgerm with yogurt, honey and stewed dried apricots and a cup of lemon herbal tea. Eat the meal slowly so that you can savour each mouthful.

9.30am Go for a brisk 30-minute walk.

11.00am Have a glass of water and then do some deep breathing.

1.00pm Lunch – a jacket potato filled with spaghetti hoops and two tomatoes. Finish with an apple.

2.15pm Practise some self-hypnosis. Have a glass of herbal tea.

4.00pm Time for some pampering – treat your feet to a foot mask.

6.00pm Prepare the evening meal. Perhaps try a vegetable curry tonight.

7.00pm Time for hibernation.

8.00pm Have a pleasant luxury bath and then get ready for an early night.

Don't forget: As you complete each activity, tick it off on your chart and before you go to sleep remember to record in your diary how you felt, noting down both the good and the bad points.

Remainder of the week

The remainder of the first week should more or less follow the pattern established here, but remember to add different foods and try some different exercises. If you feel a little bored by day 6, do something totally out of character – you're allowed to! How about buying yourself a huge coloured ball and persuading a family member or friend to have a game of 'Pass The Ball' in the garden, or see how many times you can bounce it in the air. Not only are you getting exercise, but you're having fun too. Sometimes mad moments like this are great for de-stressing the mind and body.

Exercise diary

It is a good idea to keep an exercise diary. Make a note of the activities you have undertaken and how you felt afterwards and you will soon begin to see clear signs of improvement in stamina and fitness. Fill it in at the end of each day and by the end of the programme you will see how much more you are able to do than at the beginning.

Energy snacks

While on the 28-day energy programme, you may well find yourself feeling peckish from time to time, or experiencing withdrawal symptoms from the lack of sugar in your diet. In this case it is always a good idea to have some nibbles on hand which can help stave off those hunger pangs and raise energy levels.

All the following are good energy snacks:

- Bananas
- Dried fruit
- Fresh fruit
- Nuts – brazil, flaked almonds, pecans, pine, walnuts
- Raw vegetables
- Oatcakes
- Pumpkin seeds
- Rice cakes
- Sunflower seeds

Instant energizers

When you are stressed, your breathing will almost inevitably quicken. It becomes shallow and in doing so prevents the lungs from taking in a full quota of oxygen. This ultimately leads to tiredness. To remedy this there are several instant remedies:

- Sit still for several minutes, breathing in through the nose slowly for a count of four and then out through the mouth for a count of four.
- Shake your hands vigorously from side to side.
- With the forefinger and thumb, massage around the rims of both ear lobes.

Energize: Days 8–14

By now you will have established a routine and perhaps made some changes to personalize the programme to suit your lifestyle. So are you ready for week two?

6.45am Kick-start the body with a glass of hot water and add a squeeze of lime juice.

7.15am Spend 10 minutes stretching and flexing.

8.00am Take an energy shower or bath, slapping the skin before towelling yourself dry.

8.45am Time for breakfast. Mix a chopped banana and a small pot of low-fat yogurt with some unsweetened muesli.

9.30am Buy yourself a skipping rope and spend 20 minutes skipping – remember to warm up gradually. Do not skip on a very hard surface as it may put strain on joints and muscles.

11.00am Have a glass of water and take time to do some quality breathing.

1.00pm Lunch. A chicken salad might be nice.

2.15pm Why not hire a comedy video or treat yourself to an afternoon at the cinema if there is a comedy showing. It's good to laugh. Take some dried fruit for snacking.

4.00pm Have a glass of fresh juice and do an instant energizer (see page 63).

6.00pm Evening meal. Maybe burgers tonight.

7.00pm Give your hair a home-made conditioning treatment.

8.00pm Hibernate for 20 minutes before getting an early night with a good book.

Don't forget: As you complete each activity, tick it off on your chart. Before you go to sleep, remember to record in your diary how you felt, writing down both the good and the bad points.

Remainder of the week

The remainder of week 2 should follow the same basic routine more or less. Once again, vary what you eat and your schedule for the following day – adding subtle changes will help to ensure that you don't get bored.

Avocado hair conditioner

This recipe is suitable for all hair types.

- Take one avocado.
- Remove the stone from the avocado and mash the flesh into a soft pulp.
- Massage the mixture into the hair and scalp.
- Cover the hair with a plastic bag and leave it for a full hour.
- Shampoo and rinse as normal.

Energize: Days 15–21

You are halfway there! Take a moment to congratulate yourself and then get ready for week three. You have probably established quite a fixed routine by now – remember to add changes and variations to the daily schedule to keep things fresh.

6.45am Kick-start the body with a glass of hot water and add a squeeze of lemon juice.

7.15am Spend 10 minutes stretching and flexing.

8.00am Take an energy shower or bath, slapping the skin before towelling yourself dry.

8.45am Time for breakfast. Start today with a muffin topped with fat-free cheese and a glass of freshly squeezed orange juice.

9.30am Do some gardening, or pop along to the shops, making sure you walk there and back briskly.

11.00am Have a glass of herbal tea and spend 20 minutes meditating.

1.00pm Try a new lunch dish today.

2.15pm Practise a session of self-hypnotism. Afterwards, sit down, relax and read a book or listen to some music.

4.00pm Have a glass of fresh juice and do an instant energizer.

6.00pm Evening meal. Egg fried rice is good.

7.00pm If you've had a busy day, your eyes may be feeling tired, so treat them to some pampering (see the eye revival recipe).

8.00pm Spend time quality breathing. If you are feeling peckish, eat a piece of fruit and watch some TV before going to bed.

Don't forget: As you complete each activity, tick it off on your chart. Before you go to sleep, remember to record in your diary how you felt, writing down both the good and the bad points.

Remainder of the week

Keep up with the routine even if on some days you don't feel like it. If you really feel down in the dumps, do something positive to break the mood. Go along to your local gym for a workout, and don't forget that a good dose of brisk housework or gardening is just as beneficial as a 35-minute swim in the pool.

Eye revival recipe

For puffy tired eyes.
- Take a quarter of a cucumber and one teaspoon of powdered milk.
- Grate enough cucumber, to measure approximately two teaspoons in quantity.
- Add one teaspoon of powdered milk.
- Mix together so it forms a paste. Apply it to both eyelids and also along the lower part of the eye socket.
- Leave it for ten minutes before sponging off with damp cotton wool.

Energize: Days 22—28

This is it! You are nearing the end of your 28-day Energize programme and you have survived. You should begin to feel more energetic now, largely on account of a healthier diet combined with regular exercise and relaxation. So don't give up now. Why throw away all your hard-won gains?

6.45am Kick-start the body with a glass of hot water and add a squeeze of lemon juice.

7.15am Spend 10 minutes stretching and flexing the body.

8.00am Take an energy shower or bath, slapping the skin before towelling yourself dry.

8.45am Time for breakfast. Scrambled egg on rye bread.

9.30am Go for a brisk walk and work up a sweat.

11.00am Have a glass of herbal tea and spend five minutes concentrating on quality breathing.

1.00pm Lunch – pitta bread and beans is delicious.

2.15pm Go into town and buy yourself a brightly coloured T-shirt or perhaps a bright new plant as a reward. Make sure that it is bright and cheerful. Sit down and have a glass of water when you get home. If you are feeling peckish, have some nuts.

4.00pm Time for 20 minutes hibernation.

6.00pm Evening meal. You might decide to go out for dinner to celebrate your success. Remember to choose healthily. After dinner go to the pictures and, if it's not a comedy, then perhaps see a weepy. Often a good cry is as relaxing as a good laugh.

10.00pm Bed and the sleep of the just!

Don't forget: As you complete each activity, tick it off on your chart. Before you go to sleep, remember to record in your diary how you felt, writing down both the good and the bad points.

Remainder of the week

Keep up with the routine right through to the very last day. On the final day why not celebrate, and treat yourself to some new exercise clothes? If you are feeling really good, from now on exercise will become part of your daily life.

Activity Record Chart

Record your activities every day using this table

DAILY ACTIVITIES	1	2	3	4	5	6	7	8	9	10	11	12	13	14	15	16	17	18	19	20	21	22	23	24	25	26	27	28
Glass of hot water and lemon or lime juice																												
Stretch and flex																												
Energy shower																												
Breakfast																												
Lunch																												
Dinner																												
One dose of aloe vera																												
1.75 litres (3 pints) water																												
Multivitamin supplement																												
3 portions of fresh fruit																												
3 servings of vegetables																												
1 portion non-dairy product																												
20 mins hibernation																												
10 mins self-hypnotism																												
30 mins exercise																												
Pampering																												
5 mins breathing																												
Laugh																												

Congratulations!

You've done it! You've successfully completed the 28-day Energize programme. You will probably feel healthier now than you have done for ages and very proud of yourself too.

Not only have you succeeded in eating more healthily, but you have also learned how to energize your body by exercising. You'll now know much more about your own body than you ever thought possible.

There have almost certainly been moments in the last 28 days when you felt unable to go on, but you didn't let those moments of self-doubt stand in your way and you should be very proud of yourself. And now that you have achieved this peak of good health, make sure you hold on to it.

After all, you are the only person who can make sure that you do!

To keep energy levels high:
- Avoid refined foods, such as white rice, sugar and bread
- Cut out stimulants, such as coffee, chocolate or sugar
- Eat regular small meals and healthy snacks throughout the day
- Increase your intake of complex carbohydrates – brown rice, wholegrains and seeds – which release energy slowly and steadily
- Include a protein food, such as chicken, fish or, for vegetarians, quorn or tofu with each meal
- Don't skip breakfast

Things to keep doing after the programme is over:
- Keep up with some form of regular exercise
- Make time each day for yourself, even if it is only 10 minutes
- Learn to relax

The 28 Day Plan

CELLULITE BUSTER

Cellulite

Do you suffer with cellulite? Those areas of puckered, dimpling skin on the upper part of the thighs or buttocks which, no matter what you have done, refuse to budge? Don't worry – eight out of ten women are affected with this unsightly problem, even the rich and famous who always look so perfectly groomed.

Sadly there are no 7-day wonder creams that can make it vanish or miracle cures that can eliminate it, unless you have the finances to pay for Ionithermie or Caci treatments at beauty salons. However, the good news is that with time, effort and determination you can do something about it yourself and if you follow this 28-day programme, you will end up with the smoothest, sexiest legs on the beach this summer!

What is cellulite?

To understand what you are dealing with it is important to know what cellulite is and how it is formed. Firstly, cellulite is not fat.

Although there are varying theories from different experts, the one fundamental point upon which they all agree is that it must be assumed it is a hormonal factor, because the condition largely affects women. And the guilty party has been pinpointed down to oestrogen – the more there is present in the body, the higher the probability of cellulite developing.

Before placing all the blame on oestrogen, remember that it does have an important role to play in preparing the female body to receive an embryo, and if there is an egg to fertilize the amount of oestrogen drops. Scientific studies have found that women in general now have far more oestrogen in their bodies than ever before. Unfortunately cellulite is created when there is an overload of oestrogen-causing waste matter being transported away from various organs.

Simultaneously, as this build up of oestrogen is pushing the waste away, we are eating foods that contain great amounts of preservatives, chemicals and additives which add to the excess waste already present in the body. The result is overload and sluggish circulation, and help is needed.

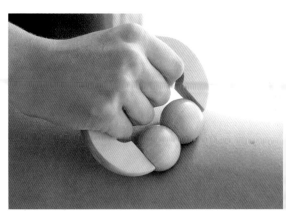

Cellulite – the facts
- Cellulite is not flab and it is not fat
- Over 95% of women have some cellulite on their bodies
- It very rarely appears in men
- In France, cellulite has been accepted as a genuine medical condition for the last 40 years
- It is not related to the size of the person – even top models get it

How to recognise cellulite

You will know you have cellulite by lightly pinching or pressing an area of tissue at the top of your thighs between your finger and thumb. Normal fat appears fairly smooth, but cellulite will reveal dimples, described as the skin of an orange. Strangely enough, cellulite tissue is also more sensitive and can often feel cold when touched and may appear whiter than other parts of your skin.

So now you know how it is formed and how to test whether you have it, you are likely to be more interested in discovering how to get rid of it. But first of all, there are other possible contributory factors to the formation of cellulite to be considered.

Bad diet: poor eating habits, too much caffeine or alcohol, and spicy foods can all cause the formation of cellulite because the toxins they produce get trapped in the fatty tissue.

Smoking: bad news all round, not only for the skin and lungs but for the damage it brings to the connective tissue that causes the dimpling effect of cellulite.

Lack of water: water is the body's best friend, especially those with cellulite. As well as re-hydrating the body, it helps flush out toxins and accumulated waste from the system. It is important to drink at least 6-8 glasses each day, more if you can.

Lifestyle: those who are employed in office jobs and spend all day sitting at a desk are more prone to the development of cellulite due to an overall sluggish circulation, especially in the buttocks and thigh areas. Try to get up every hour or so and have a walk around, even if it is just a visit to the loo. And at lunchtime, make sure you go out for a walk.

Lack of exercise: exercise is the best thing you can do for your body. It improves muscle tone, circulation and overall well being, helping to break up blocked tissue and purify the blood.

How to get rid of cellulite

In order to deal with cellulite it helps to understand a little of our fat anatomy. Beneath the surface of the skin there is a thin layer of subcutaneous fat whose role is to cushion the body against a sudden trauma. It also keeps the body warm. Delve deeper and there is another layer of fat called the scarpus fascia that controls the bumps and various bulges in our body. This is the dreaded area where fat cells lurk and which enlarge as we gain weight. But it is also subdivided into chambers via connective tissue which holds the top layer of skin to those layers underneath. Once the connective tissue weakens and misshapes, it pulls on the surface of the skin and thus creates the dimpled effect on the skin called cellulite.

How to help yourself

We've already mentioned there are lots of costly treatments and various creams that are purported to eradicate cellulite from the body but the problem is, they can be expensive and, furthermore, do they actually work?

Why spend money when you can have the knowledge at your fingertips and by following a combination of diet, dry skin brushing, massage and the use of certain essential oils you can deal very effectively with cellulite yourself.

Diet: experts recommend people with cellulite follow a detoxifying diet that includes eating plenty of fresh fruits, vegetables and whole grains. Not only will it cleanse and detoxify the entire system, thus enabling

Remember, cellulite loves:
✗ Sitting around too much
✗ Processed and refined foods
✗ Coffee
✗ Alcohol
✗ Neglecting one's body
SO DON'T DO THEM!

Remember, cellulite hates:
✓ Exercise
✓ Low-fat diet
✓ Lots of water
✓ Regular beauty pampering
✓ Skin brushing
SO DO THEM!

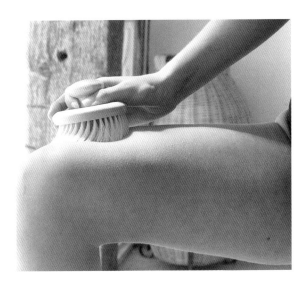

toxic wastes to be eradicated, but will prevent further cellulite forming.

Dry skin brushing: a highly effective method for stimulating the hard particles of matter in the lymphatic system, which hinder the elimination of the toxins from the system.

Aromatherapy: the therapeutic benefits of using essential oils in the treatment of eradicating cellulite have long been recognized.

Relaxation: stress and worry make cellulite worse by releasing extra adrenaline into the system and causing the liver to work overtime by eradicating the excess. Spend time relaxing and deep breathing, allowing your lungs to fill with oxygen and thus greatly improving the circulation.

Massage: if you go to a beauty salon for professional treatment of cellulite you will probably find they use a combination of aromatherapy and massage known

as lymphatic drainage massage – a hard kneading of the skin which pummels and works away at the cellulite deposits at the same time as activating the lymph nodes. You can learn to do this at home (see Daily Treatments).

Things that can make cellulite worse:
• Tight clothing
• The contraceptive pill: experts believe the release of complex biochemical substances into the body can interfere with the body's metabolism and help cause the formation of cellulite
• Sunshine: the dimpling effect may be made worse by sunbathing since excessive exposure to the sunlight is known to cause the skin to lose its elasticity

Exercising Cellulite Away

Cellulite just loves the person who doesn't exercise, who'd far rather take the car to the shops and whose one and only physical activity is to climb the stairs to bed! This has got to change if you want to banish that cellulite.

Just take a look at female athletes and see how toned and lean their legs are without a sign of puckered skin. The reason is their active lifestyle doesn't give cellulite a chance to settle, and you can be like that too by including a disciplined exercise routine into your programme.

Home exercises

Would you like your legs to look well toned with not a glimmer of cellulite and be able to flaunt them off

at the beach in your brand new bathing costume? Here is a selection of stretching and toning exercises that will help you achieve that dream, and which can be done in the comfort and privacy of your own home.

Remember, before you begin do some gentle warming up exercises to flex and stretch the muscles and thereby prevent any possible injury. Gentle jogging on the spot followed by some stretching exercises should suffice. And when the routine is complete, do the same cooling down exercises to return the heart rate to normal.

Plan to do three exercise sessions a week, each lasting 30 minutes. But if this is too much, split the routine into three 10-minute sessions spread throughout the day.

It is all a matter of choice, just do what feels right for your body and don't over exert yourself. Exercising should be fun.

Before starting any exercise programme you should see your GP if you:
- Have been inactive for some time
- Are a woman aged over 50
- Suffer heart or lung disease, high blood pressure, diabetes, arthritis or asthma
- Are a smoker
- Are overweight
- Are pregnant
- Are concerned in any way about your health

Hip and thigh exercises

Choose three of the following and repeat them 10 times daily:

Squat

A great exercise for the thighs and buttocks

1. Stand with feet hip-width apart, with the left foot 45-60cm (18-24in) behind the right one and slightly bent at the knee.
2. Keep both arms by your sides. Keep back straight and head up with chin parallel to the floor.
3. Slowly bend both legs and lower your body. Take it easy and don't worry if you can't do it the first few times. Just concentrate and do the movements in your own time. Stop if you feel pressure on your knees.
4. Change sides to work the other leg.

Inner thigh toner

1. Lie on the floor on your side, with one arm supporting your head.
2. With the lower leg bent and resting on the floor, raise the top leg off the floor as far as you are able without straining, hold and then gently lower it back to the floor.
3. Once you have done one side, turn over and work on the other leg.

Bottom toner

1. Lie on your front, hands resting on top of one another, chin resting lightly on top.
2. Raise one leg about 12.5cm (5in) off the floor and hold for a count of 10.
3. Slowly lower the leg back to the floor and repeat with the other leg.

Hip toner 1

1. Stand sideways with your hand resting on a chair, knees slightly bent, shoulders relaxed.
2. Slowly raise your right leg, making sure you keep both your body and raised foot facing forwards.
3. Carefully and slowly lower your leg.
4. Turn around and repeat with the other leg.

Hip toner 2

1. Stand facing the back of a chair. With both hands resting on the chair, stand with knees slightly bent, shoulders relaxed.
2. Slowly raise your right leg out to the side, making sure you keep both your body and raised foot facing forwards.
3. Carefully and slowly lower your leg.
4. Repeat with the other leg.

Lunges

These are ideal for working on the thighs and buttocks and perfect for doing at home. If you feel you need weights, grab hold of a couple of cans of beans.

1. Place hands on hips and stand up straight. Alternatively, hold a weight in each hand and stand up straight with palms facing in towards your body.
2. Place your feet hip width apart. Keep head up with chin parallel to the ground.
3. Take one step forward, slowly bending both knees so the front knee aligns with the ankle and the rear heel is lifted.
4. Don't allow your back knee to touch the floor
5. Push yourself back up. Stop if pain occurs in knee joints or ligaments.
6. Alternate this action on the other leg.

Housework and related duties can burn up various amounts of calories:
- Climbing the stairs burns up 10 calories a minute
- Vacuuming can burn up 6 calories a minute
- One hour's worth of digging in the garden can burn up 392 calories

Upper arms

If you find that you have traces of cellulite on the backs of upper arms, try this exercise.

1. Fill a 3-litre (5-pint) empty plastic pop bottle with water to use as a weight.
2. Sit on a seat.
3. Take the bottle in one hand and move it over your head, palm facing inwards.
4. Slowly bend your elbow so that you are bringing the bottle down to your shoulder but without altering the upper arm position.
5. Lift the arm up and repeat the same process again.
6. Do this exercise six times with one arm and six with the other.

Stomach exercises

It is worthwhile doing a few pelvic lifts before you to any stomach exercises. Pelvic lifts help to strengthen and protect the muscles that run under your pelvis from your pubic bone through to your bottom.

Pelvic lift

You can do this standing, with legs parallel, hip-width apart, or lying on your back on the floor with knees raised, feet flat on the floor hip-width apart. Contract the muscles that you would use to stop the flow of urine, hold for five seconds then relax and repeat five times.

This is an exercise which can be performed standing almost anywhere at any time.

Tummy crunchers

1. Lie on your back with your knees bent and your feet flat on the floor, hip-width apart.
2. Tilt your pelvis until your lower back is pressed flat against the floor.
3. Rest your hands lightly against the side of your head.
4. Now slowly lift your head and shoulders a little way off the floor.
5. Hold for a few seconds and then lower back down to the floor.
6. Repeat 15–20 times.

Exercising outside

Sometimes exercising in the house can get a little boring, so why not go outside for a change or combine your exercise programme with some outdoor activities?

If you find choosing an appropriate exercise a little difficult, the best ones for dealing with cellulite are those that will help firm and tone up the legs, hips and bottom. Ideally aim to work out for between 20-40 minutes each time and as your stamina increases, then you can build on to the time.

Cycling: the ideal exercise for firming the fronts and backs of your thighs.

Tennis: there is no better exercise than tennis for promoting shapely legs.

Power walking: according to experts you don't have to work up a sweat at the gym on a workout to tone up your muscles – a brisk walk is just as good. In fact the medical profession agrees that the health benefits associated with walking exceed those of every other form of exercise.

Power walking can:
- help you shape up and at the same time burn approximately 350 calories an hour
- lower cholesterol
- regulate blood pressure
- relieve chronic pain
- help insomnia and infertility
- alleviate depression

Different kinds of exercise burn up various amounts of calories:

Walking: if done for 30 minutes burns up 230 calories

Cycling: if done for 30 minutes burns up 192 calories

Swimming: if done for 20 minutes burns up 180 calories

Skating: if done for 20 minutes burns up 207 calories

Dancing: if done for 25 minutes burns up 215 calories

Aerobics: if done for an hour burns up 306 calories

What better all-round form of exercise could you ask for? To get the full benefit, aim to do three or four 20-minute sessions of brisk walking a week. The technique is simple: shoulders back, neck relaxed, shoulders aligned directly above your hips and a heel-toe roll in a straight line through the foot narrowing the width of your track to allow for greater speed with arms and legs moving in sync. Each week try to improve on your last efforts by going a little further. Always warm up and cool down before and afterwards.

Aerobics: no better exercise for strengthening and toning the legs as well as the rest of the body. Join in a local gym.

Step classes: these help to sculpt the legs but make sure you don't do more than one class a week otherwise you will risk bulking up your legs too much.

Spinning: one of the latest fitness crazes. The classes entail riding really quickly on a special exercise bike while the instructor keeps you pedalling with different techniques and music. A 45-minute workout can apparently burn up an amazing 500 calories. Your local gym may well have more details.

Water: if you exercise in water, it is 15 times more effective than doing that same exercise on land simply because of the resistance against your muscles. Water is a superb and quick way to tone your body because whichever direction you move, your body will still have to push against the water.

Skipping: indoors or outdoors, skipping is the ideal all-over workout and perfect for stretching the leg muscles. It also works the heart, lungs and upper body to get a really good workout. You may have to start in bursts of 2-3 minutes but you will be pleasantly surprised how quickly the body adapts.

Spare minute exercises
Here are two simple exercises that can be done in any spare moment – whilst washing the dishes, waiting in the bus queue, even when serving dinner!
Bum clencher Clench your buttocks, hold for a few seconds and then simply release – perfect for toning up the buttocks.
Thigh firmer When waiting for the kettle to boil, gradually raise and lower your leg straight behind and as high as you can, almost like a ballerina. Hold the position for 30 seconds and then repeat with the other leg.

Helpful Treatments

There are lots of other treatments that can help deal with banishing cellulite and will therefore prove invaluable included in the programme, each of which have their own benefits.

Your daily routine every day until the third week should be skin brushing, aromatherapy, and massage. After the third week use the massage oils every alternate day.

Dry skin brushing

Skin brushing is one of the most effective and cheapest ways of encouraging the drainage of excess fluid from those areas of the body prone to cellulite. In order for it to be truly effective and enable the lymphatic system to clear itself and expel waste, it must be done on a daily basis, often for several months, and applied with a special brush with hard and scratchy bristles. Five minutes of dry skin brushing per day can:

- improve digestion
- aid metabolism
- impart new levels of energy
- dissipate cellulite

How to do it

Give yourself an overall body brush and feel the overall benefits. Begin by brushing your fingers and hands. Hold your fingers outstretched and brush in between them several times before moving on to the hand, and then the palms before doing the other hand.

Using long strokes, take the brush from the wrist to the elbow and then from the elbow to the shoulder. Remember to use long, firm, bold strokes and always brush towards the heart to encourage the blood flow.

Feet and toes are next. Resting one leg on the side of the bath or a chair, sweep across the toes and then the soles of the feet, moving around the leg and up from the ankle. This should be done approximately 14 times.

The thighs and buttocks are next. When you brush the thighs work upwards, as vigorously as you can, concentrating on the areas where cellulite is particularly evident. Finally, brush the buttocks firmly in any direction. Generally, skin brushing should be performed in the direction of the heart, but circular movements around the buttocks are best. After working on the lower body, graduate up to the neck and brush downwards from the head to the shoulders.

The front and sides of the body are next. Don't brush over the nipples but gently applying pressure around the breasts is fine. Don't brush the stomach and abdomen but move on to the back, using long firm strokes.

Don't expect miracles overnight – you will probably need to do this at least every other day to be most effective, although some people do it every day. Never brush over broken skin. If the skin is red and scratched after brushing, the next day take it a little more gently.

Aromatherapy

For many people aromatherapy oil means something they add to their bathwater as an aid to relaxation. There are hundreds of different essential oils, each with their own inherent properties and you can easily learn how to use some of them in your programme.

There are various special anti-cellulite oils on the market, based on the principles of aromatherapy, which are a combination of essential oils diluted in correct carrier oils and you are advised to buy them from a health shop where you can ask advice. Remember to check if your chosen oil is suitable for application to the skin once diluted in carrier oil. This is especially important if you are pregnant.

How to use essential oils

After body brushing, shake three or four drops of essential oil into the bathwater and soak for about 20 minutes. During this time take in deep breaths. As you lie in the bath knead and pummel the cellulite areas.

Once out of the bath and dry, massage some diluted oil into each thigh and the buttocks, paying particular attention to those cellulite areas. You may also wish to rub some diluted oil over your stomach and so increase detoxification. This treatment is best performed either first thing in the morning or early evening.

Yoga

It may sound rather odd thinking that yoga can help deal with cellulite, but those who practise yoga fervently very rarely suffer with it. It seems that all the stretching and flexing of muscles activates the circulation of blood and other fluids around the body.

It may be a good idea to see if there are any local yoga classes to join or why not visit the library to borrow some yoga books and a video to do at home.

Essential oils said to be effective anti-cellulite oils:

- Black pepper
- Clary sage
- Cypress
- Geranium
- Juniper
- Lemon
- Patchouli
- Rosemary
- Sandalwood

Self massage

In any successful cellulite programme massage is an important element. Daily massage will help you learn to identify those areas where cellulite has formed and you will also come to know your body in a different way. At the beginning do it every single day by body brushing first and then follow with a massage.

Massage is fundamental in dealing with the reduction of cellulite as it:

✓ encourages circulation and can stimulate blood flow

✓ improves digestion

✓ increases kidney function

✓ flushes out the lymphatic system by the elimination of toxins and waste

How to do it

Select an appropriate essential oil and pour a small amount into the palm of your hand and, using long stroking movements, begin at the ankle and work up to the knee and thigh using both hands, massaging the oil in well and making sure the movements are gentle but firm.

Experts recommend the best type of massage when dealing with cellulite is kneading, adopting the same action as though you were kneading dough. As you pick up the flesh you squeeze it, applying as much pressure as possible, almost as if you were punching areas of flesh.

Rolling is another useful movement for cellulite sufferers. This is where you pick up about an inch of flesh on the thigh and roll the flesh to break down the deposits.

After a time you will be able to identify those areas that contain more cellulite as they feel hard and grainy and as you apply pressure you will experience a ripple sensation.

Kneading and pinching at the flesh is something that you can do anytime and anywhere – when you are sitting watching television or waiting for the kettle to boil.

Detox bath

An Epsom salts bath is cheaper than many of the shop-bought preparations which contain seaweed and sea extracts which help eliminate toxins and fluid retention. Simply add 225-450g ($^1/_2$-1lb) of Epsom salts to a hot bath and soak in it for 15 minutes.

Wrap up well afterwards and drink plenty of water as you will continue sweating and eliminating toxins for an hour or two. Try to rest for an hour after bathing.

Warning: Do not do this if you are pregnant or have heart problems.

Body scrubs

In order to improve the skin's texture and tone it up, body scrubs are worth including in the programme and should ideally be undertaken either before or during a shower, as they can be rather messy.

Scrubs involve massaging the skin with a gritty substance to remove dead skin cells and engrained grime and improve the overall appearance of the skin. They can either be used on their own or with a rough flannel or loofah to increase their effectiveness.

Body scrub recipe
50g (2oz) crunchy peanut butter
25g (1oz) finely ground sea salt
30ml (2 tablespoons) almond oil

Mix the peanut butter and sea salt together and stir in the almond oil to form a soft paste. Rub on to damp skin all over the body, paying greater attention to hard areas on the elbows, upper arms and knees. Rinse off with warm water, then have a shower.

Healthy Eating Plan

Dealing with cellulite isn't just about exercise. It is also about adopting a healthy eating plan, knowing which foods are better than others and eradicating those bad foods from your diet.

Unfortunately today's modern diet is a minefield for the cellulite sufferer due to its high sugar and fat content and with greater emphasis on processed and refined foods as opposed to fresh, natural ingredients. In truth, the body is a garbage bin to so much junk and rubbish that our liver, kidneys and bowels often find dealing with it too much. Once they have reached their capacity for elimination, the only alternative is for the waste to remain in the system.

Changing eating habits does not mean following a diet or calorie-counting, but it does mean watching that you eat healthy, nourishing food with a balance of essential nutrients derived from the following:

- Carbohydrates
- Proteins
- Fat
- Vitamins
- Minerals

Carbohydrates: these provide energy for the body and come in two types: simple carbohydrates which include basically sugar and very little else, and complex carbohydrates which include starchy foods such as bread, potatoes, cereal, pasta, rice, etc.

Protein: the body breaks down the protein from food into its component building blocks called amino acids that it then uses to build and repair tissue and muscle. Found in foods such as meat, poultry, fish, dairy foods such as cheese and yogurt, eggs, beans, lentils and nuts, cereals, etc.

Fat: number one enemy for the body but essential for helping to insulate and protect the organs and nerves. It is found in varying quantities in numerous foods such as butter, cheese, lard, dripping, snack foods, fatty meat, etc. The basic aim of a healthy diet is to reduce the amount of fat you eat and stick to a low-fat diet; it doesn't mean cutting them out totally, simply choosing those foods sensibly and checking on the label for low fat.

A healthy eating programme

The major part of a healthy eating programme consists of fresh fruit and vegetables, largely because of their abundance of minerals and vitamins. Canned and processed foods are best avoided as they contain additives and preservatives, but if you do find yourself having to eat some then make sure the greater proportion of that meal is salad or lightly steamed vegetables.

High in calories, nuts are also high in fibre, nutrients and potassium so are the ideal source of essential unsaturated fatty acids. Best eaten raw, unsalted and fresh.

Just as nuts are high in nutrients, so too are pulses and seeds and once fully sprouted their nutrient content increases. Great for adding flavour and colour to foods.

Fish is the perfect food as it contains all the vital

proteins. But as with most food, it is healthier eaten fresh rather than frozen which will be depleted of many essential nutrients. Smoked fish is fine provided it has been treated naturally. Avoid eating fish in brine as it is too salty. If selecting canned fish, those in olive or vegetable oil are the best.

Good foods for banishing cellulite

Fruit
- Apples
- Apricots
- Bilberries
- Blackberries
- Blackcurrants
- Blueberries
- Cherries
- Cranberries
- Currants
- Damsons
- Dates
- Figs
- Gooseberries
- Grapefruit
- Grapes
- Greengages
- Guavas
- Kiwi fruit
- Lemons
- Limes
- Loganberries
- Lychees
- Mangoes
- Melons
- Mulberries
- Nectarines
- Passionfruit
- Paw-paw
- Peaches
- Pears
- Pineapple
- Plums
- Pomegranates
- Prunes
- Quinces
- Raisins
- Raspberries
- Redcurrants
- Rhubarb
- Strawberries
- Sultanas

Vegetables
- Artichokes
- Asparagus
- Aubergines
- Beans (broad, butter, haricot, mung, runner, French, red kidney)
- Beansprouts
- Beetroot
- Broccoli
- Brussels sprouts
- Cabbage, (red, savoy, spring, white, winter)
- Carrots
- Cauliflower
- Celeriac
- Celery
- Chicory
- Chinese leaf
- Courgettes
- Cucumber
- Fennel
- Kohlrabi
- Leeks
- Lettuce
- Marrow
- Okra
- Onion
- Parsnips
- Peas
- Peppers (bell, capsicum)
- Plantain
- Potatoes
- Pumpkin
- Radishes
- Spring greens
- Spring onions
- Squashes
- Swede
- Sweetcorn
- Sweet potatoes
- Turnips
- Watercress
- Yams

Nuts
- Almonds
- Brazils
- Cashews
- Chestnuts
- Hazelnuts
- Macadamia nuts
- Pecans
- Pine nuts
- Pistachios
- Walnuts

Seeds, pulses and herbs
- Alfalfa
- Basil
- Cardamom pods
- Cayenne pepper
- Chillies
- Coriander
- Chickpeas
- Dill
- Fennel
- Ginger
- Lemongrass
- Marjoram
- Parsley
- Pepper
- Pumpkin seeds
- Rosemary
- Sage
- Sesame seeds
- Sunflower seeds
- Tarragon
- Thyme

Fish
- Cod
- Crab
- Haddock
- Halibut
- Herring
- Lemon sole
- Lobster
- Mackerel
- Monkfish
- Pilchards
- Plaice
- Prawns
- Salmon
- Sardines
- Scampi
- Shrimps
- Skate
- Trout
- Tuna

Non-dairy foods
- Goat's cheese/milk/yogurt
- Sheep's milk/cheese/yogurt
- Rice milk
- Soya milk

Reduce certain foods

The main aim of the diet is to enable the body to detoxify itself by eliminating long-held waste. It is not intended to be a weight-reducing diet, nor is it specifically intended as a diet only suitable for those who have cellulite to lose. The key word in fighting cellulite is purification not weight loss, and so it is important that whilst purifying the system you avoid certain foods:

Helpful tips

It isn't only cutting out certain foods or including others that will help in your cellulite plan but equally important how you eat and how you prepare food:
• When choosing something to eat, consider its nutritional value and not only its taste
• Stick to regular mealtimes and try not to snack in between meals
• Eat slowly and chew your food thoroughly
• Do not drink liquids at mealtimes, as they tend to dilute the digestive juices therefore making it more difficult to digest food.
• Maintain an adequate water intake during the day.
• If eating fish, boil or bake it
• Avoid adding gravies, salad dressings and other rich sauces to your food. A healthier option is to mix a little oil with vinegar or lemon juice.
• Check on the label that the food is low fat

Planning Food

Whilst on the ban-the-cellulite programme, make sure that each day you try to eat:
✓ Three portions of vegetables
✓ Three portions of fruit
✓ Three portions of salad
✓ One portion of non-dairy yogurt, cheese or milk
✓ Two portions of nuts or fish
✓ One portion of brown rice

Drinking

Maintaining a healthy balance of fluids is always essential when cleansing out the system. Aim to drink at least 1.75 litres (3 pints) of water a day and if drinking plain water becomes a little boring, you can always add lemon, lime, honey or even ginger.

Fruit juices: these can be drunk in addition to the required amount of water, but if buying pre-packed check on the label that it is pure, unsweetened fruit juice and not the variety made up in water from fruit pulp. But better still, if you have a juicer you can make your own.

Herbal teas: there are lots of different varieties in supermarkets such as camomile, aniseed, dandelion, ginger and fennel.

Drinks to avoid:
• Alcohol
• Fizzy drinks
• Tea
• Hot chocolate
• Coffee

Dining out

A quick word about dining out whilst on the cellulite buster programme.

- Always have a glass or two of water before the meal to avoid eating too much and feeling bloated.
- If having a starter, choose vegetables and then if you are still peckish follow it up with a green salad.
- And just on the odd occasion you can have a special treat and choose a dessert.
- Try to stick with salads or vegetarian meals. Vegetable curries with rice are fine. Avoid naan bread because it contains raising agents and preservatives – remember you are trying to eat natural foods whenever possible.

Cellulite loves:
- ✗ Processed food
- ✗ Fizzy drinks
- ✗ Coffee
- ✗ Alcohol
- ✗ White bread

Cellulite hates:
- ✓ Lots of water
- ✓ Low fat foods
- ✓ Fresh fruit
- ✓ Fresh vegetables

Daily Treatments

To enable the programme to be successful there are certain things to follow each day, especially when detoxing the body.

Important foods and liquids

Hot lemon water: beginning the day with a hot cup of water and a squeeze of lemon or lime juice will freshen your mouth and give the liver a kick start – the largest organ involved in detoxing.

Water: cleansing, restoring and rejuvenating are the three basic principles in a detox programme and the one important thing which can help these three successfully is water. So make sure you drink plenty.

Liver tonic: the liver should be treated with kid gloves throughout the 28-day programme in order to do its job efficiently. To help do this, it needs a tonic in the form of at least two of the following foods each day:

• Two cups of fennel or dandelion tea
• A medium glass of pure carrot and beetroot juice
• A medium bunch of grapes
• Include a fresh clove of garlic in your food

Kidney tonics: as with the liver, the kidneys also have a hard job to do in detoxing and including certain foods in the diet will enable them to work more efficiently. Each day you must take two of the following:

• Sip a teaspoon of fresh honey dissolved in a cup of hot water
• A medium glass of cranberry juice
• Half a medium melon

Supplements: whenever changes in eating habits are made, they often affect the metabolic rate and if sufficient quantities of foods are not ingested, the body begins slowing down. At the beginning of your programme you may find it worthwhile to include certain supplements such as kelp, which equips the body with adequate amounts of iodine needed for balancing the metabolism and ideal to use when detoxing.

Vitamin supplements: it may be a good idea to include an all-round vitamin supplement in the initial stages of your detox programme to make sure the body is not being depleted of any essential nutrients. Generally, after two weeks, the body has adjusted and so you can stop taking them.

Whilst on the programme make sure each day you:

✓ Drink a cup of hot water and lemon/lime juice each morning
✓ Drink at least 1.75 litres (3 pints) of water during the day
✓ Take two liver tonics
✓ Take two kidney tonics
✓ Take a kelp supplement
✓ Take a multivitamin supplement for the first 15 days
✓ Eat three meals a day
✓ Eat one portion of rice (preferably short brown grain)
✓ Eat three portions of vegetables (one of which should be raw)
✓ Eat three portions of fruit
✓ Eat three portions of salad
✓ Eat one portion of non-dairy produce

Don't forget the outside

Just as you have dealt with the internal system cleansing and flushing out of poisonous toxins, you should begin to look outward and consider your overall wellbeing. The only way a programme can be termed a success is if both the outside and inside have been cleansed with a combination of exercise, relaxation and pampering.

Take a shower

Refreshing, invigorating and rejuvenating, an early morning shower is just what the body needs to jump-start it into action. But just as you are nearly finished, turn the cold tap on allowing the cold water to run over your body for one minute. It might sound a little barbaric but it will:

✓ tone up the skin
✓ tone up the muscles
✓ give the lymphatic system a jump start

Have a cold bath

This may sound a little harsh but in the second or third week try taking a cold bath. Experts advocate that they:

✓ ease menopausal side effects
✓ re-energize
✓ boost immunity
✓ reduce the risk of heart attack
✓ increase fertility

Simply run a cold bath, walk up and down in it to boost your circulation then take a deep breath and sit down waist deep for 3-5 minutes to cool the lower part of your body. Finally, for the brave hearted, submerge yourself up to your neck for 10-20 minutes, moving your limbs gently from time to time. Get out and briskly rub yourself dry. Wrap yourself in a snug blanket for at least 20 minutes to allow your body to recuperate. This is perhaps best done in the afternoon.

Each day throughout your cellulite-busting programme:

✓ Drink a glass of water each morning with a squeeze of lemon or lime juice added
✓ Take a cold shower/bath
✓ Do some dry skin brushing
✓ Take 30 minutes exercise
✓ Spend 5-10 minutes on acupressure
✓ Spend 5 minutes on quality breathing
✓ Take an Epsom salts bath every 5 days

Drink

Don't forget that early morning glass of water with an added squeeze of lemon or lime to kick start the body into action, cleanse your mouth and put a zing in your step.

Exercise

Exercises designed to tone and strengthen the abdominal area are recommended and form a very important part of the daily programme. As your stamina increases, gradually build up the number of repetitions you do. After the first week you may feel like taking up some outdoor exercises for a change.

Deep breathing

There is nothing quite so invigorating or relaxing as five minutes of deep, steady breathing to blow away those cobwebs. If you are wearing a skirt or trousers, undo the waistband so there is ample space for you to expand your stomach. Deep breathing is also excellent for helping to de-stress.

1. Sit in a quiet room.
2. Close your eyes and slowly breathe in, holding that breath to the count of five, then to the count of five slowly exhale through your mouth.
3. Repeat again several times.

Maintaining The Programme

Trying to change is never easy and there are bound to be occasions throughout the 28 days when you think why bother, what is the point of it all?

This programme isn't meant to be an ordeal – a little hard work perhaps, but not something you dread doing and so it is important to set aside an hour or so each day for some tender loving care.

Pamper yourself
You may well encounter negative days while on this programme which is why it is important always to have something to look forward to. If you feel low, spend a day with friends, treat yourself to something, visit the hairdresser or listen to your favourite music.

Exfoliate
In order to clear the skin of dead skin cells and freshen it up, a regular facial scrub does it the world of good. Don't just use a facial scrub over the face; remember the elbows and knees also benefit from this beauty treatment. Rinse thoroughly with tepid water.

Quick oatmeal scrub: Make up a paste of oatmeal and water, then apply it to the face. Once it has dried and the skin feels tight, rub it off using your fingers to clean away all the dead skin cells. Rinse thoroughly with tepid water.

Wheatgerm exfoliator: This is ideal for all skin types. Mix together 1 tablespoon of wheatgerm with 1 tablespoon of single cream in a bowl until they form a paste. Massage it gently over the skin, and then rinse clear with tepid water.

Epsom salts bath
Speed up the elimination of toxins from the skin and improve its circulation with an Epsom salts bath. Run the bath water and add 225-450g (^{1}/$_2$-1lb) of Epsom salts. Soak for about 20 minutes, and when you get

ut, keep yourself warm by piling on lots of clothes – this will help the body to continue sweating out the toxins. Most chemists and health food stores sell Epsom salts.

Olive oil treatment

Can't afford a trip to the hairdresser but your hair feels in need of some attention? Try an olive oil treatment. Put some olive oil into a bowl and warm it gently over a saucepan of water. When it is warm but not too hot, apply it over the hair and massage well into the scalp. Leave it on for 15 minutes, then shampoo thoroughly.

Scream

Do you often feel like having a good scream, shouting and yelling like a banshee until all that pent-up emotion and frustration inside has been expelled? So what are you waiting for? Go for it! Just make sure you don't frighten anyone else with your actions. You'll feel so much better afterwards. Another equally good method for 'letting it all out' is to punch some pillows!

Acupressure techniques

When you feel completely stressed and worn out, you may well benefit from a little acupressure, a common term for a technique that uses pressure in order to arouse certain energy points throughout the body. In doing so, it corrects any imbalance, moves any energy blockages and helps treat specific aliments. It was first discovered by the Chinese over 5,000 years ago and is something that you can do in your own home.

Practise it up to five times a day. Do not practise it if you are pregnant or have a medical condition.

To help ease exhaustion: Using the thumb and forefinger of one hand, apply pressure on the point in the middle of your little finger on the other hand, just

below the top bone. Hold for 20 seconds before slowly releasing and repeat again four times, waiting 10 seconds between applying the pressure.

Balneotherapy

Have you ever tried balneotherapy? It is so relaxing if practised once a week and involves immersing yourself in a bath at a temperature of just below 32°C for 20 minutes. Add some seaweed powder (available at health food shops) and you will find it lowers your blood pressure, boosts metabolism and aids elimination of toxins from the body.

Days 1–7

You've done all the preparatory work and so can look forward to the following 28-day programme. By the end of it you should feel invigorated and rejuvenated.

Whether you are a working woman or a busy mum, the next 28 days will include some big changes in your life, so be prepared. Make up a chart (see page 97) and stick it on your kitchen wall so that you will remember what you must include each day in your programme.

Don't forget to keep a diary to record your everyday thoughts. Even if you have had a rotten day, write it down and then try to understand why it was such a bad day.

Here is a typical plan for day one, but naturally times will differ and the order in which activities are done may also change according to your individual lifestyle and work commitments.

7.15am Wake up and have a glass of water with a squeeze of lemon juice.

8.00am Get the circulation moving and give your body a dry skin brush. Then jump into the shower – don't forget to turn on a blast of cold water before you come out.

8.45am Breakfast – on the first day opt for some fresh fruit such as papaya or pineapple and eat it slowly. Complement it with a cup of herbal tea.

9.15am Start the day the way you mean to end and do some power walking.

11.00am Time for relaxation and quality breathing. Have a glass of water afterwards and sit down to listen to some music.

1.00pm Time for lunch. Try a salad today with a lemon dressing. Finish off with a piece of fruit.

2.15pm Why not try an exercise routine for the stomach area.

4.00pm Time for some pampering and recuperation after the exercising, so make some of your own lip balm – it's so easy to do (see recipe).

6.00pm Prepare dinner.

7.00pm De-stressing. It's been a hard day and you have made many changes, so sit in a quiet room and do some acupressure.

8.00pm Have an aromatherapy bath. Put some candles around the room, add some of your favourite essential oils, then relax. Then have an early night.

Don't forget – as you complete each activity, tick it off on your chart and before you go to sleep remember to record in your diary how you felt, both the good and bad points. Then write down what you intend doing the following day, or prepare the food you intend eating.

Remainder of the week

The first week of anything new is always the hardest, so be kind to yourself. Making changes is never easy so do them gradually. Instead of going out, stay in and do a workout programme. Spend one morning cooking a batch of meals to pop into the freezer so you won't have to worry about what you are going to eat. You won't notice many changes in the first week so don't be too impatient.

Strawberry lip balm

A simple lip balm that is easy to make. You can replace the strawberry essential oil with any other, if you wish.

2 tablespoons petroleum jelly
1 teaspoon beeswax
12 drops strawberry essential oil

Melt the petroleum jelly and beeswax in a small bowl over a pan of boiling water. Add the strawberry essential oil, stir well. Transfer into a small container and leave to set.

Measurements chart

As you change your routine and reform your eating habits, you will find that you are not only banishing cellulite but looking good and feeling better. You will have toned up muscles all over your body to give you a slimmer look and lots more energy!

You can record your measurements each week using this simple chart.

	Week 1	Week 2	Week 3	Week 4
Date				
Weight				
Bust				
Waist				
Hips				
Thighs				

Days 8–14

With the first week over, certain routines should be established, but remember no slacking and no adding in foods that are banned!

7.15am Have a glass of water with a squeeze of lime juice

8.00am Get the circulation moving and give your body a dry skin brush. Then massage the skin before having a shower.

8.45am Breakfast. During this week you can have something more substantial for breakfast. So how about porridge made with water instead of milk.

10.15am Do the full exercise routine this morning. Repeat each of the hip, thigh and stomach exercises ten times. This should take at least 30 minutes – don't rush it and work at your own speed.

11.15am Time for relaxation and quality breathing. Have a glass of water afterwards and sit down to listen to some music.

1.00pm Time for lunch. Always finish off with a piece of fruit.

2.15pm Be a total water baby today and go along to your local swimming pool for an hour. If 20 minutes' swimming burns up 180 calories, just imagine what an hour's worth will use up.

4.00pm You've had a busy day so you will need some relaxation. Why not give yourself a facial and see how relaxed you feel afterwards. See face mask recipe.

6.00pm Prepare dinner. Tonight have a salad with lots of fresh vegetables and some fruit.

7.00pm Another tiring day, so why not have a cold

bath to wake your system up.

9.00pm Remember that comedy video you bought and haven't had a chance to watch, well there is no time like the present and you will fee so totally relaxed that when it has finished you will be ready for bed.

Don't forget - as you do each activity, tick it off on your chart and before you go to sleep remember to record in your diary how you felt, the good and bad points.

Remainder of the week

Add in different exercises or borrow a yoga video from the library and begin studying it. Try out some different recipes using the foods that you are allowed. And remember to keep kneading at that cellulite.

Honey and grape face mask

Take a handful of grapes, 1 tablespoon honey, 1 egg yolk and 1 teaspoon olive oil. De-seed and skin the grapes. Pop all the ingredients into a liquidizer. When blended thoroughly, apply to the face. Leave for 15 minutes, then rinse off with warm water. The honey moisturizes the skin while the egg yolk provides it with protein and the olive oil softens it.

Days 15–21

It's the third week and by now you should start to see some slight changes. You will feel healthier and more energetic and you may well notice some changes in your skin.

7.15am Wake up and have a glass of water with a squeeze of lemon juice. Give your body a well-deserved stretch and feel totally invigorated. Lying in bed for 8 hours can cause muscular aches and pains to develop and this inactivity can ultimately lead to a build-up of lactic acid in the muscles, resulting in pain and stiffness. That is why the daily routine of stretching the arms and body is invaluable.

8.00am Get the circulation moving and give yourself a dry skin brush. Then jump into the shower.

8.45am Breakfast.

10.15am Today clean the house from top to bottom. The added incentive is that the harder you do each individual task, the more calories the body burns!

11.15am Time for some breathing exercises and follow up with a cup of herbal tea.

1.00pm Time for lunch. How about a healthy, nutritious and tasty jacket potato today?.

2.15pm Go to the shops and do some simple exercises when standing in the queues. Clench your buttocks, hold for a few seconds and then release.

4.00pm Back at home do some hip and thigh exercises before sitting down with a cup of herbal tea.

6.00pm Prepare dinner. Tonight, perhaps a salad.

7.00pm Do some meditation in a quiet room.

9.00pm Have a detox bath and then another early night.

Don't forget – as you do each activity, tick it off on your chart and before you go to sleep remember to record in your diary how you felt, both the good and bad points.

Remainder of the week

You are nearly at the end of the programme and by now you will probably be looking and feeling a whole lot better but don't start slacking. It is often towards the end when most people do stop, but unless you complete the programme you can't expect to reach your target of banishing the cellulite.

Days 22–28

This is nearly it, the end of your 28-day programme and you have survived. You should begin to feel more energetic now, largely due to a healthier diet combined with regular exercise and relaxation. So don't give up now.

7.15am Wake up and have a glass of water with a squeeze of lime juice. Get the circulation moving and give your body a dry skin brush. Then jump into the shower.

8.00am Breakfast.

8.45am Do the full exercise programme.

10.15am Have a cup of herbal tea and then sit down and relax by watching the TV or listening to some favourite music.

11.15am Get ready to meet some friends in town. Spend time putting on your make-up and choose clothes that will show off your new look.

1.00pm Time for lunch. Choose something healthy and have a glass of fresh orange juice.

2.15pm Back at home, take a cold bath and practise balneotherapy.

4.00pm Do some acupressure.

6.00pm To celebrate the end of the programme why not go out for a meal, but remember to choose your meal wisely. You are allowed one glass of wine.

9.00pm Sit down and put your feet up – you deserve it.

Don't forget – as you do each activity, tick it off on your chart and before you go to sleep remember to record in your diary how you felt, both the good and bad points.

Remainder of the week

Keep up with the routine, even to the very last day. On the final day why not celebrate and treat yourself to some new exercise clothes because from now on, a you feel so much better, exercise will become part of your daily life.

Activity Record Chart

Record your activities every day using this table

DAILY ACTIVITIES	1	2	3	4	5	6	7	8	9	10	11	12	13	14	15	16	17	18	19	20	21	22	23	24	25	26	27	28
Glass of hot water and lemon or lime juice																												
Dry skin brushing																												
Cold water bath/shower																												
Breakfast																												
Lunch																												
Dinner																												
2 liver tonics																												
2 kidney tonics																												
1 kelp supplement																												
Multivitamin supplement (15 days)																												
1.75 litres (3 pints) water																												
1 portion short brown rice																												
3 portions vegetables (1 raw)																												
3 portions fresh fruit																												
3 portions salad																												
1 portion non-dairy food																												
30 mins exercise																												
5–10 mins acupressure																												
5 mins quality breathing																												
Epsom salts bath every five days																												

Congratulations!

It was probably the hardest 28 days of your life but you have succeeded – you have banished the cellulite and proved it can be done.

It might not have been plain sailing, you may have well faltered along the way and succumbed to the occasional bar of chocolate, but that doesn't really matter provided you got back on to the programme immediately!

And just think of all the money you have saved by not going along to a beauty salon for hours of expensive treatment. It will probably be enough to allow you to treat yourself to a new bathing costume to show off those smooth long legs this summer.

But now that you have come this far, you don't want to risk dropping the routine and allowing the cellulite return. So be sensible, and add some of the changes you have adopted throughout the programme into your daily life.

Things to continue after the programme
- Exercise
- Following a healthy diet
- Make sure that you drink at least 1.75 litres (3 pints) of water a day
- Don't forget body brushing when you have a bath or shower
- And, above all, be proud of the way you look

The 28 Day Plan

GET FIT FOR SUMMER

Get Fit For Summer

Are you ready for summer? Do you feel confident enough to cast off those long jumpers and baggy trousers and slip into something more revealing, or do you cringe at the thought of exposing your less-than-lean thighs and cower in embarrassment that you didn't do something about that slight bulge lying around your midriff before now?

Don't worry, help is at hand – if you follow this 28-day programme, you too can flaunt a well-toned body on the beach this summer.

Are you fit?

Can you run upstairs without panting for breath? Take the family dog for a long walk and arrive home without feeling totally exhausted? Swim a couple of lengths at the local pool and not feel as though you had swum in the Olympics? If you can't, it looks as if you, along with many other people, are slightly unfit. However, the difference is that, simply by picking up this book, you have decided to do something about it.

Feeling fit and being fit are essentially two different things. We can't all afford the luxury of employing a personal trainer like some of the top stars to attain a wonderful sylph-like figure, but then again with a little time and effort on your part you can look just as good, if not better, even if it does entail having to forego that daily bar of chocolate or can of fizzy drink. But surely, at the end of the day, looking and feeling so much healthier is worth the initial input

Feeling fit

Good health and feeling fit mean different things to different people. It could be the ability to do things that were impossible before, taking part in physical

activities, feeling better about the way you look, feeling younger or feeling more active and alive when you wake up in the morning.

The essence of this 28-day programme is to illustrate that the secret of good health is a combined programme of healthy eating and exercise, changing bad habits for good habits, learning to listen to your body and making sure it remains at the optimum level of good health. So don't sit around poring over diet sheets; take time to work your way through this 28-day regime and find out for yourself what getting fit is all about.

WARNING
Before embarking upon this programme, it is wise to consult with your GP if you suffer from any of the following medical conditions:
- You are pregnant or breastfeeding
- You have diabetes
- Have anaemia
- Have diabetes
- Are underweight
- Are under stress
- Are taking medication that cannot be stopped

Before starting

If you are really serious, write out on a sheet of paper your reasons for wanting to get fit and set yourself some realistic goals to aim for but don't make them too extreme. Perhaps you want to go on holiday and wear a bathing costume for the first time in years, or feel confident enough to wear shorts during the summer; both are sound and reasonable targets that are achievable. When you feel fit, you automatically feel so much better about yourself, physically and psychologically:

When I get fit:
- I will look better on my summer holiday
- I will be able to wear a bathing costume
- I will be able to wear cropped tops
- My skin and complexion will look better
- I will feel more energetic and active

Did you know?
- You are technically unfit if you unable to walk 1.6km (1 mile) in 12 minutes without becoming out of breath
- If you want to get and remain fit the minimum amount of exercise required to maintain average fitness is 20 minutes three times a week

Assessing Your Diet

Do you follow a healthy, well-balanced diet? How much do you know about the food you eat? Do you read the labelling on the side of the packaging?

Did you know that at one time carbohydrate foods were the bad boys and therefore to be avoided at all costs, and yet recent research studies have revealed that a diet low in fat and high in carbohydrates is what we should aim for.

Nutritionists advise that in order for the body to function at its optimum it needs a well balanced diet which should include carbohydrates, protein, fats, minerals and vitamins. However, it is only by eating a variety of foods in sensible proportions that we can obtain the correct amount of nutrients needed to maintain good health.

The three basic rules regarding food are that:
1. It should nourish the body
2. Help safeguard health
3. Whenever possible play a role in helping fight against ailments or disease

This programme is not intended as a weight-loss diet, although some people may find that they do lose a little weight, but rather a way of demonstrating to people a healthy way of eating.

How unhealthy is your diet?
How many times a week do you eat fish and chips or grab a burger at lunchtime? What about those pre-packed frozen meals that only require a blast in the microwave for several minutes or a meal in a can, that provides a meal within minutes?

The problem is that we live in an age where everything is needed yesterday, family meal times when everyone sits around the table together are fast disappearing and eating convenient 'fast' food often seems easier than choosing the healthy option. It is hardly surprising to learn that so many people are suffering eating disorders and allergies, so perhaps the time has come to take a look at our own individual eating habits.

Bad eating habits
- Skipping meals
- Eating junk and convenience foods
- Eating between meals
- Snacking on high sugary foods
- Eating when you are sad or worried
- Eating on the go

Skipping meals: one of the biggest problems when people are in such a hurry is that they find themselves skipping meals, so they may have breakfast then not eat anything until later in the evening, surviving on a diet of coffee and a chocolate biscuit.

Convenience foods: we are a nation of fast-food junkies in that anything that is quick to prepare is fine to eat, hardly giving its nutritional value any consideration. Although ready-prepared meals do save time this doesn't prevent them losing valuable nutrients during reheating, and experts have found that convenience foods contain more sugar, salt and fat than most other foods. However, to counterbalance the argument, it must be said that there are an increasing number of 'healthy' or 'calorie-counted' meals' now available.

Fast foods: the occasional burger or meal of take-away fish and chips is fine provided it is not a diet based purely on fast foods. Although certainly of a higher quality than ten years ago, the fact is that most do contain a lot of calories and a lot of fat.

Eating between meals: most people do snack between meals; for many with little or poor appetites this is the ideal way for them to maintain their energy levels. But problems occur when snacking is largely confined to sugary or salted foods, cream cakes or crisps. If you do snack between meals, then think healthy and choose from the following list:

- ✓ Apples
- ✓ Bananas
- ✓ Handful of dried fruit
- ✓ Oranges
- ✓ Pears
- ✓ Celery
- ✓ Raw carrot
- ✓ Cauliflower florets

And remember, if you are a snack eater the frequent presence of food in the mouth can encourage the build up of bacteria that in turn cause plaque, so brush and floss the teeth regularly.

Eating when sad: many people turn to food when they are angry or sad, depressed or worried, even on some occasions when happy, but there is always an underlying factor to trigger this behaviour. It could be you have just ended a relationship, lost your job or feel under stress and food is your only ally. But when it results in putting on extra kilos when you'd much rather prefer not to, then it becomes an enemy. So if you find that you are always nibbling for no

particular reason, try to find out the cause before it gets out of control.

Eating on the go: never eat on the go. It's not healthy and it doesn't give the body time to digest the food. So if you find you are guilty of this, the simple answer is to stop!

Good eating habits

It is possible to adopt good eating habits and although it may seem you are having to give up all the things you enjoy eating, you are wrong. It doesn't mean having to forgo eating a cake or a packet of crisps, eat them by all means, but in moderation. Instead of having three glasses of wine when you go out, have one. When the family is having an apple pie and custard for their dessert, skip the apple pie and just have an apple. And if you fancy a bar of chocolate, then have the occasional small one.

Good eating habits
- ✓ Eat three balanced meals a day
- ✓ Don't snack on sugary foods
- ✓ Don't deprive yourself of everything you enjoy

What Does A Healthy Body Need?

In order to function at its optimum a healthy body needs a well-balanced diet which should include carbohydrates, protein, fats, minerals and vitamins.

Carbohydrates: the main function of carbohydrates is to provide energy for the body. During digestion carbohydrates are converted into glucose and then absorbed into the bloodstream. It is the glucose that the body uses for energy. If energy is not immediately required, it is stored in the muscles and liver as glycogen and is readily available to be converted into glucose when extra energy is required. Foods containing carbohydrates include: sugar, syrup, jam, honey, fruit, bread, puddings, cereals, potatoes.

Proteins: these are invaluable to the body for their vital role in repairing and maintaining the tissue, muscles and blood cells. An excess intake of protein is either converted into energy or transposed into fat and held in the body for emergency use. Found in foods including: meat, fish, cheese, eggs, milk, soya beans, nuts, cereals and pulses.

Fats: the role fats play in the body's energy status is to supply it with a concentrated source of energy and also essential fatty acids, vital for maintaining healthy skin and the regulating body

functions. Found in foods including: milk, butter, cream, cheese, suet, fatty meat, oily fish, margarine, salad or cooking oils.

Vitamins: important for healthy functioning of cells. Present in small amounts in all foods, a varied, sensible diet including a high proportion of fresh fruit and vegetables will ensure a sufficient intake for good health although some vitamin loss occurs during cooking. Foods containing high levels of vitamins include fresh fruit and vegetables, milk, butter, cheese, eggs, margarine, fish.

Minerals: inorganic substances found in foods from both animal and vegetable sources and required in very small quantities. They are essential for the repair of tissues, healthy formation of bones, teeth and blood cells, maintenance of body fluids and metabolic functions. Foods high in mineral content include dark green leafy vegetables, sardines, liver, kidney, egg yolk, yogurt, milk and cheese.

Achieving a balanced diet

Health authorities in Britain and the United States have drawn up guidelines for healthy eating. There are five identified by the British Health Education Authority, whilst six appear in the four-tier US food pyramid. The American pyramid differs from the British model only in that it places fruit and vegetables into separate categories. The other four groups are shared by both and include the following:

Six daily servings of complex carbohydrates.
Including bread, cereals, potatoes, pasta, rice and noodles.
• Choose wholemeal brown or high fibre breads, increase your intake by making thicker sandwiches but with less filling. Eat bread with main meals and have a larger helping of potatoes, rice or pasta rather than higher fat foods.
• Don't fry any of the foods in this group.
• Don't spread butter or margarine thickly on bread.
• Don't add cream or rich sauces or oily dressings to these foods.

Five daily servings of fruit
This includes fresh, frozen and canned fruits, fruit juice and dried fruit.
• Select a wide and varied range of fruits and have more than one as a dessert by making up a bowl of fruit salad. Add fruit to a sandwich filling. Make a fresh fruit or vegetable drink.
• Don't, however, eat excessive amounts in one sitting as this could lead to indigestion.

Five daily servings of vegetables
This includes all types of vegetable.
• Use tomatoes and other vegetables, fresh or frozen, in sauces or serve as a traditional side dish or with meat or pasta.
• Don't deep-fry vegetables – they will soak up the oil.
• If stir-frying, do so in a little oil which is healthier.

Two daily servings milk and dairy products
This includes semi-skimmed milk, cheese, yogurt, calcium-enriched soya milk.
• Eat only moderate amounts, choosing reduced fat versions such as semi-skimmed milk or low-fat yogurt (always check the labelling before buying).
• Don't consume large amounts of full-fat varieties of cream, milk, cheese or butter.

Two daily servings of protein
This includes oily fish, lean meat, chicken, turkey and fish.
• Eat moderate amounts of these foods, choosing only those that are lean with all visible fat trimmed. Try eating fish at least twice a week and include some oily fish such as mackerel or salmon.
• Don't fry meat or fish.
• Don't add fat to those already rich in oils. Instead grill, poach, steam, stir-fry or even roast – all are healthier cooking methods.

Two daily servings of fats
This includes margarine, butter, chocolate, crisps, biscuits. pastries and sweets.
• Choose lower fat brands or eat only small amounts, using spread and oils sparingly. Skim any fat from meat juices when making gravy.
• Don't be tempted to eat more than one chocolate or fill yourself up between meals with sugary snack foods or high fat snacks such as crisps.

Little treats

You can eat as much fruit as you like – it's a convenient snack food, packed full of goodness and available in many different shapes, sizes and flavours.

But we all need a little extra sweet treat now and then:

Bread and jam: there's nothing like a slice of bread and jam and you can still indulge, provided you chose wholemeal bread and choose a low-sugar jam.

Chocolate: in moderation chocolate can be healthy. It can provide a good proportion of an adult's daily copper intake, necessary to help create red cells and strengthen bones.

Cheese: nutritious but some varieties are high in fat and should be eaten in moderation. But if you enjoy eating cheese with a meal, try those with a lower fat content such as cottage cheese, ricotta or fromage frais.

inger and carrot cake

 teaspoons ground ginger

 75g (6oz) dark brown soft sugar

 25g (8oz) self raising flour

 large carrots, washed and grated

 egg, beaten

 50ml (8fl oz) skimmed milk

'reheat the oven on to 190°C/350°F/gas mark 4. Line
 450g (1lb) tin with greaseproof paper. Blend the
 round ginger, sugar and flour into a bowl. Add in the
 rated carrots and stir. Add the egg to the milk and
 tir this into the mixture, blending in well. Pour the
 nixture into the prepared tin and bake in the oven
 or approximately 55 minutes, or until a skewer
 nserted into the cake comes out clean. Leave to cool.

Healthy eating tips

 his programme isn't about losing weight, nor is
 about calorie counting. It is about looking at ways to
 at healthily and curb any bad eating habits you may
 nave adopted over the years.

 Drink lots of sparkling water – it fills you up, keeps
 you hydrated and helps flush waste products from
 your body. Aim for at least 8 glasses a day.

 Don't overeat – get into a habit of eating slightly
smaller portions and if you still feel hungry, wait
10 minutes before returning for a second serving.

• Eat plenty of plant-based foods such as fruit, grains
and vegetables as they're packed with nutrients.
Include lean protein foods too, but only low-fat dairy
products in small amounts.

• Habits are difficult to break but it isn't impossible.
Eating on the go or, worse still, eating from the bag is
hardly going to do your digestive system much good.
So make a rule to only eat at the table with a knife
and fork.

• Don't drink your calories – chewing takes longer
and ultimately provides more satisfaction. Instead of
drinking a glass of orange juice, why not eat an
orange instead?

When following this 28-day programme:
• Eat regularly and enjoy your meals
• Eat a wide variety of foods
• Eat enough to maintain your weight and height
• Eat plenty of foods rich in carbohydrate and fibre
• Don't eat too much fat
• Don't eat sugary foods too often
• People with special dietary requirements and those
  under medical supervision should check with their
  GP to see if this balance of foods is suited to them.

• If you drink alcohol, keep within the sensible limits
• Use only moderate amounts of salt in cooking and
  don't add salt to your meal
• British nutritionists recommend we should drink
  1.5-2 litres (3-4 pints) of fluid a day to maintain
  health liquids. Most of this should be made up
  of water.
• Ensure you get plenty of vitamins and minerals in
  your diet (perhaps take a supplement each day)

Healthy Meals

If you are looking for some tasty meals for your new eating routine, here are some suggestions you may like to try.

Breakfasts

• Bowl of muesli with fresh fruit, followed by a slice of wholemeal toast with a little butter or low-fat spread and marmalade.

• Bowl of cornflakes topped with a grated apple and served with skimmed or semi-skimmed milk, plus a glass of fresh unsweetened orange juice.

• Bowl of cornflakes with several strawberries and skimmed or semi-skimmed milk

• Two slices of wholemeal bread filled with grilled lean bacon

• One poached egg on a slice of toasted wholemeal bread

Haddock omelette

This is great for the weekend when you have more time to prepare a special breakfast.

3 egg whites

Salt and pepper

Spray bottle of light oil

50g (2oz) smoked flaked haddock

1 small tomato

2 slices of wholemeal bread

Whisk up the egg whites and season with salt and pepper. Spray a shot of light oil into a non-stick frying pan and, when it is heated through, pour in the egg mix. Shake the pan well and cook the egg whites. Remove the pan from the heat, and add the flaked haddock, then pop them under the grill for 3 minutes. Meanwhile, halve the tomato and grill it. Toast the bread. Turn the omelette onto a plate and serve with the wholemeal toast and the tomato.

Kiwi smoothie

A treat for those who prefer to drink their gourmet breakfast.

4 kiwi fruits

1 small banana

Lemon juice

Small carton low-fat natural yogurt

Peel the kiwi fruits and the banana. Add them into a blender with a dash of lemon juice and the yogurt. Once blended, pop some ice into a glass and pour the smoothie over.

Lunch

If you have the time here are some ideas for nutritious lunchtime recipes you can try. Some of them could be prepared the evening before and stored in the refrigerator.

Mackerel toasties

Something to rustle up in a few minutes. Drain a can of mackerel fillets and put them into a bowl. Mash them up with a fork and stir in a teaspoon of mustard and some chopped spring onions. Lavishly spread the mixture over two slices of wholemeal toast and pop under the grill for a few minutes until warm.

rumstick supreme

very easy recipe which makes tasty lunchtime treat.

clove garlic, peeled and crushed
teaspoon dried oregano
teaspoon dried thyme
teaspoon dried rosemary
5g (1oz) breadcrumbs
alt and pepper
chicken drumsticks
tablespoons low-fat natural yogurt

op all the ingredients, except the drumsticks and
ogurt, into a plastic bag and give it a good shake.
sing a very sharp knife carefully pierce the
rumsticks then cover liberally with the yogurt. Pop
he drumsticks into the bag and give another good
hake, making sure they each get well covered with
he ingredients. Remove from the bag and place each
nder a pre-heated grill for approximately15 minutes,
urning them once. The drumsticks are ready to eat
vhen no pink juices trickle out when pierced with a
kewer.

spanish omelette

*A delicious lunchtime snack that can be served
1ot or cold.*

tablespoon olive oil
medium onion, peeled and sliced
clove garlic, peeled and crushed
/2 pepper, red, green or yellow
450g (1lb) new potatoes, cooked and diced
4 eggs, beaten
Salt and pepper

Pour the tablespoon of olive oil into a frying pan and
sauté the sliced onion and garlic. When just turning
golden brown, add the potatoes. When browned, add
the eggs, salt and pepper and cook slowly until firm.

Spicy chicken

*This is the ideal lunchtime dish when you have friends
calling around, as the quantities will serve four.*

1 large chicken, cut into four pieces
Salt and pepper
1 teaspoon curry powder
Pinch of celery salt
$1/2$ teaspoon ground ginger
150ml (5fl oz) low-fat natural fromage frais
1 teaspoon paprika

Wash the chicken and season the inside with salt and
pepper. Mix the curry powder, celery salt and ground
ginger together, then add it to the fromage frais.
Place the chicken in a microwave-proof dish. Pour the
fromage frais mixture over the chicken and then
sprinkle with paprika. Pop it into the microwave on
high for 8 minutes per 450g (1lb). Leave it to stand
for 15 minutes before serving. The chicken is ready to
eat when, pierced with a skewer at the thickest part,
the juices run clear; if still pink then cook for a little
longer and test again.

Dinner

Mealtimes can a problem when you run out of ideas, but there are lots of delicious meals you can prepare with a little thought and ingenuity that will appeal to all the family.

Chilli con carne

A great family dinner, serving four.

450g (1lb) lean minced beef
1 large onion, peeled and chopped
400g (14oz) can chopped tomatoes
2 bay leaves
1 teaspoon Bovril
425g (15oz) can red
   kidney beans
1 teaspoon chilli
   powder
2 cloves garlic, peeled
   and crushed
Black pepper

Dry-fry the mince in a non-stick frying pan, then drain it through a colander. Clean any fat from the frying pan, then add the onion and dry-fry it. As the onion is turning brown, return the mince to the pan together with the tomatoes, bay leaf, Bovril, kidney beans, chilli powder and garlic. Season with black pepper. Cook for about 10 minutes, stirring occasionally and adding a little water if it becomes too thick. Serve with brown boiled rice.

Chicken celebration

Serves four.

Black pepper
4 chicken breasts, skinned
225g (8oz) brown rice
450g (1lb) canned beansprouts
Soy sauce

Sprinkle a preheated non-stick frying pan with black pepper, then add the chicken and sauté until it begins to turn brown. Generously sprinkle the chicken pieces with more black pepper before turning over on to the other side to cook. Cover the pan with a lid, turn the heat down slightly and leave the chicken gently simmering for a further 20 minutes, checking every 5 minutes or so and turning the chicken over to cook on the other side.

Whilst waiting for the chicken, cook the rice in boiling water and drain. Pop the rice and drained can of beansprouts into a colander and pour a kettle of boiling water over to reheat them. Drain and tip onto a serving dish, placing the chicken pieces on the top and adding an extra tang with a dash of soy sauce.

Chicken risotto

Serves four.

25g (1oz) low fat spread
225g (8oz) skinless chicken, cut into small bite sizes
1 green pepper, de-seeded and
   finely chopped
1 small onion finely chopped
1 clove garlic, crushed
Herbs to season
700ml (1³/4 pt) chicken stock
275g (10oz) long grain brown rice
1 tablespoon lemon juice
275g (10oz) mushrooms, sliced
Tomato slices to garnish

Melt the low fat spread in a large pan and add the chicken, pepper, onion, garlic and seasoning. Cook for 5 minutes. Add the stock, rice and lemon juice continue cooking with the lid on over a medium heat for 20 minutes. Add the sliced mushrooms and cook for a further 5 minutes. Serve garnished with slices of tomato and a mixed green salad.

trawberry sorbet

Jealthy, nutritious and a perfect source of Vitamin C.

50g (1 lb) fresh strawberries, washed and hulled

Juice of 1 large orange

ut the strawberries into a food processor with the
range juice and blend. Pour the mixture into a bowl
nd pop into the freezer for 1 hour. Remove and leave
it to thaw slightly, then beat with a metal spoon and
return to the freezer for a further 5 hours.
o appreciate the taste, the sorbet should
ie left to soften at room temperature for
20 minutes before serving.

Melon delight

150g (16oz) melon

275ml (10fl oz) low-fat flavoured yogurt

225g (8oz) green grapes

Chop up the melon flesh and separate it
equally between 4 tall glasses then spoon
generous amounts of yogurt over the top.
Cut the grapes in half and share them
between the glasses. Spoon the rest of the
yogurt over the top and pop into the
freezer to chill.

**If you feel peckish at any time during
the day, avoid that tempting chocolate
bar or packet of crisps and eat a low
calorie snack of healthy fruit or
vegetables. Choose from:**

- An orange
- An apple
- Handful of grapes
- A banana
- Handful of cherries
- Dried fruit
- Cauliflower florets
- A carrot
- A stick of celery
- A pear

**Desserts provide the finishing touch to a delicious
meal but avoid eating anything too heavy. Try the
following ideas:**

- 1 meringue nest filled with 115g (4oz) fresh fruit
  and topped with 50g (2oz) low-fat yogurt
- 2 pieces of fresh fruit
- Diced apple and pear with low-fat yogurt

Daily Exercises

There are four main reasons why most people become bored with exercising: lack of time, no local gym, boredom, absence of results.

Lack of time: if you really want to do something, you will make time for it. And just imagine how much benefit you will gain from exercising – you will feel fitter and healthier, have a reasonable level of fitness and be better equipped to deal with stress. Besides, you don't have to take part in a marathon or go jogging – exercising can amount to a brisk walk, doing some gentle workout exercises at home, or even gardening.

No local gym: there's no need to enrol at a gym – you could rent a keep fit video or go for a swim at your local pool.

Boredom: this is a popular excuse, or is it just an excuse for opting out? There are lots of ways you can make exercising more fun – exercise at different times of the day, ask a friend to join in or work out to some music. You could also enrol at an activity class at you local college.

Absence of results: if you set yourself small goals an then keep a diary recording what you have achieved and how you feel, you will then spot those small changes that may have otherwise gone unnoticed.

Before you begin your new programme

If you have recently given birth, have been inactive for several years or suffer from any of the medical conditions listed below, then you should, for your own safety, consider making an appointment to see your GP before beginning an exercise routine.

- High blood pressure
- Heart trouble
- Family history of early stroke or heart attacks
- Frequent dizzy spells
- Extreme breathlessness after mild exertion
- Arthritis or other bone problems
- Severe muscular, ligament or tendon problems
- Other known or suspected disease

Exercises for specific areas of the body

There are exercise routines to help tone up all parts of the body and if you have one particular area that you feel needs more work than another, then simply spend more time working on that. But if you are looking for an all-round tone up exercise regime, try this routine every day which takes approximately 20 minutes. Make sure that you drink plenty of water.

Warm up

It is essential before any workout routine to spend 5 minutes warming the muscles up.

1. Stand with the feet apart and swing the arms forward and down between your legs, bending the knees as you do but keeping the back straight.

2. Straighten your legs, swing your arms back up to the stretched position.

3. Inhale as you stretch, and exhale as you curl down.

4. Repeat as fast as you can 20 times.

Arms and chest

An ideal exercise for trimming upper arms and lifting the chest.

1. Stand with both feet hip width apart and arms down by your sides, holding a light weight (such as a can of beans) in each hand.

2. Bring the arms slightly forwards, raise the hands, then bend and lift the elbows up and back, pushing hard.

3. Lower the arms back down and repeat 30 times.

Stomach and waist

1. Stand with feet hip width apart, arms down by your sides and still holding on to the weights, raise the arms to shoulder level, then bend the elbows.
2. Punch the right hand hard to the right, twisting the body round at the same time so the hips are front-facing.
3. Return to the standing position and this time punch your right fist to the left, twisting the body around as much as possible. Repeat 20 times.
4. Repeat the same sequence but this time with the left hand. Repeat this 20 times.

You may find it more comfortable if you use a thin workout mat for the floor exercises.

Thighs

This tones and strengthens thigh muscles.
1. Stand with feet hip width apart and hands resting on the hips.
2. Put the right leg forward and bend the knee, with the left leg back and knee bent, almost touching the floor.
3. Jump into the air, crossing the legs so the right leg comes forwards and the left leg goes back.
4. When landing, allow the knees to bend then jump and cross the legs over again.
5. Repeat 20 times.

Stomach

1. Lie down on the floor, with hands by your sides, both palms facing down and feet together.
2. Slowly raise both legs vertically.
3. Lower the right leg almost to the floor, then as you begin to raise it again, lower the left leg almost to the floor. Both legs should cross in a scissor position.
4. Repeat 10-20 times.

Hips, buttocks and legs

1. Continue lying on your back on the floor, arms spread horizontally, palms down.
2. Raise the left leg as high as possible, making sure it is kept perfectly straight.
3. Move the foot towards you, cross the leg over to touch the floor on your right side, reaching as high up your body as you are able to. Keep legs straight and shoulders touching the ground.
4. Repeat with your right leg in the same way.
5. Repeat 10 times.

Cool down

Lie on the floor, relax and rest for one minute, allowing your body to cool down and your heart rate to return to normal.

Other exercises

If you feel you really haven't the time to spend 20 minutes on a workout, then just do what you are able to.

Exercises for the middle body

This is ideal for working on those flabby abdominal muscles.

1. Lie on your back with, knees bent and feet hip width apart on the floor.
2. Bend your elbows and place your hands behind your ears so that your fingertips touch.
3. Move your chin so it is in alignment with the rest of your spine and move your elbows slightly inwards.
4. Pull in your abs gently towards your spine.
5. Curl slowly upwards and forwards until the head, neck and shoulders are clear of the floor. Hold that position for a count of ten, then slowly lower and then repeat.

For the back area

1. Lie on your stomach, arms and legs outstretched.
2. Tilt your head forward so it is resting on the floor or, if more comfortable, rest it on the side.
3. Lift your right leg and right arm a few centimetres off the floor and stretch them out towards opposite ends of the room.
4. Hold for one minute, then slowly lower them back down to the starting position.
5. Repeat with the other arm and leg.

For shoulders and arms

1. Kneel on the floor with your weight in your hands.
2. Pull in your abs so that your back doesn't sag.
3. Bend your elbows and lower your body down towards the floor.
4. Once your upper arms are almost parallel with the floor, press back up to the starting position, hold and then repeat.

Exercises for the reluctant keep-fitter

If you have been working all day, then possibly the last thing on your mind is doing anything more physical other drinking a cup of tea. But it is still quite possible to tone and trim muscles even when sitting on the sofa.

Head

Look directly in front and extend the back of the neck up and towards the ceiling whilst easing the shoulders down, keeping your jaw parallel with the floor. Hold for 5 seconds and repeat the other side.

Shoulders

Ease both shoulders forwards and upwards, then back and down. The secret is to move through each new direction in one continuous circle, say it out loud: forward, upwards, backwards, downwards, making the circle as large as you are able.

Waist

1. Sit upright on a chair or stool with legs and feet hip width apart, knees directly over the ankles.
2. Put your arms at chest level, bent at the elbows with forearms resting on one another.
3. Twisting from the middle, slowly turn your head shoulders and arms around to the left as far as possible, keeping your shoulders down throughout this move.
4. Return to the starting position and repeat the other side.

Energetic exercising

Exercise that makes you sweat a little is perfect for the battle of losing weight and is known as 'aerobic' exercise, covering any activity that you can do for long periods of time. Your own personal level of fitness will partly determine the type of exercise you take part in, but it is important not to push yourself. Go at your own pace and increase your workout gradually. If you feel ill, dizzy, faint or in any way poorly, you must stop any exercise and check with your GP before taking it up again.

The main aim is to work out for 20-40 minutes each time, building up gradually, as you become fitter. Alternatively, break your sessions up into 10-minute routine. The long-term effect of exercise is that you will build up the amount of muscle in your body and decrease the amount of fat. The more muscle you have, the more food you are able to eat without gaining weight.

Fact

Every 450g (1lb) of muscle in your body burns off 35 calories a day.

Aerobic activities cover a wide range
- Badminton
- Dancing
- Kickboxing
- Power walking
- Rowing
- Skipping
- Swimming
- Tennis
- Water aerobics

Daily Treatments

To achieve ultimate success on the programme – a healthier, fitter body – it is important that you include each of the following treatments in your 28-day plan.

Daily treatments
- Start the morning with a drink of hot water with a dash of lemon juice
- Take a daily energy shower
- Spend 30 minutes exercising
- Take a brisk 30-minute walk
- Spend 20 minutes in hibernation

Extra treatments
- Every week give yourself a salt scrub
- Every three days have a salt bath

Hot lemon water: begin the day with a hot cup of water and a squeeze of lemon/lime juice. This will freshen your mouth and is good for helping to cleanse the system.

Energy shower: there's nothing like an early morning energy shower to kick-start the body into action, so the first thing each morning jump into the shower and, if brave enough, when you are ready to come out, turn the cold tap full on for several minutes.

Exercise to energize

Keep these three words firmly focused in your mind's eye. Write them in large print on a piece of paper and pin it up in the kitchen or bathroom so whenever you feel sluggish you can remind yourself.

If you haven't exercised since the day you left school, apart from walking to the shops, then you are bound to feel a little apprehensive. But all the experts advocate that a daily dose of activity helps our emotional and physical wellbeing and actually increases energy levels by releasing endorphins which are the body's natural high hormones and make you feel great. When you first begin exercising, take it easy – don't overdo it and gradually build up. By the end of the programme exercising will form part of your daily routine.

Walk

Make a determined effort each day to go for a walk, even if it is just to the shops. Try to walk for at least 20-30 minutes because walking:

- Helps stabilize blood sugar levels and therefore helps to avoid mood swings
- Can alleviate stress, tension and depression due to those 'feel-good' hormones it triggers
- Is an ally against the development of osteoporosis because it is a weight-bearing exercise
- Combined with healthily eating there is no better way to help fight the flab
- Strengthens the heart
- Speeds up mental alertness
- And can even help and cure back pain by building up the muscles that stabilize the spine

Hibernation

It is amazing how a daily 20-minute mini-break can restore depleting energy resources and recharge flagging batteries. Just take yourself off somewhere, perhaps to a quiet room or out in the garden, where you can feel totally relaxed and allow yourself to 'switch off' for 20 minutes. Think about no one and nothing but peace and tranquillity.

Body scrubs

In order to improve the skin's texture and tone it up, body scrubs are well worth including in the programme and should ideally be undertaken either before or during a shower, as they can be rather messy.

They involve massaging the skin with a gritty substance to move dead skin cells and engrained grime and improve the overall appearance of the skin. They can either be used on their own or with a rough flannel or loofah to increase their effectiveness.

Body scrub recipe: For an inexpensive scrub mix a handful of sea salt with a dollop of olive oil, leave for

a few minutes to give the salt time to dissolve slightly, then rub it all over the body and rinse off.

Salt bath

Bathing in a solution of Epsom salts is good for the skin as it draws out toxins through the pores. Run the bath water and add 225-450g (^{1}/$_2$-1lb) of Epsom salts. Soak for about 20 minutes, and when you get out, keep yourself warm by piling on lots of clothes. This will help the body to continue sweating out the toxins.

Don't be surprised if you are feel thirsty afterwards – it is the effect of sweating which causes this. Just make sure you drink lots of water.

Salt baths are not advisable if you have:
- Heart or kidney problems • High blood pressure

Maintaining The Programme

Often the most difficult part in following any programme is preventing boredom from setting in. This is why it is important to integrate some little treats into your programme.

Do something totally wild and out of character – spend an afternoon at a funfair and relive your childhood days, book yourself on a bus trip for a day, surf the net, call up an old friend, have a wardrobe or make-up blitz and get rid of all your old clutter to make way for the new you.

Think calm

We all get days when we feel totally stressed and agitated, but a few minutes spent relaxing can calm away those tensions and frustrations and help you put things into perspective. One useful trick is to inhale essential oils. Fill a large bowl with boiling water and add two drops each of clary sage, rosemary and geranium essential oils. Lean your head over the bowl (not too close or you risk scalding yourself) and trap the steam by draping a towel over your head. Now close your eyes and breathe deeply for 5 minutes.

Rest

During part of the day, if you feel particularly stressed or anxious for no apparent reason, try to take yourself off somewhere peaceful, go into another room and listen to some calming music or do a short relaxation exercise.

• Sit in a comfortable position, close your eyes and breathe in through your nose.
• Feel the breath reach deep down into your lungs.
• Exhale slowly through your mouth and remain still for a few moments listening to the sound of your breath.

• Become aware of your body relaxing.
• Begin with the muscles of your scalp and face and slowly work down your body, releasing all the tension as you go.
• Concentrate on your favourite colour and then picture it in its brightest form. Imagine it turning darker, then visualize it dancing around and creating patterns.
• Slowly allow the colour to drain away and watch as it becomes paler and paler until eventually it disappears.
• Disregard any thoughts that may creep into your mind whilst concentrating, brush them aside and keep firmly focused on your colour.

Meditation and relaxation aren't always easy to master but they are worth the effort. Several minutes of inner silence on a regular basis will provide you with an experience to last a lifetime. Make time each day to relax and relieve the tensions in your body and allow your mind to be free from daily worries. Don't force yourself – if at first it doesn't work, wait a couple of days and then try again.

Be creative
Why not do something creative – write a poem, paint a picture, write a letter to a friend.

Singing

Many people who suffer from panic attacks find that singing loudly makes them feel better. Singing helps you breathe more deeply, giving your body the oxygen it needs to get you back in control.

Blitz the make-up

With a new healthier lifestyle and a trimmer body, surely the time has arrived to throw out some of your old make-up. Spend an afternoon at the local beauty section of your department store where the staff are always willing to give you advice on the best colours or shades to suit your skin. Some will give you a free make-up too.

Exfoliate the skin

The skin cells generally renew themselves every 3-4 weeks, but as you get older this process slows down and you can end up with a dull, lifeless complexion. Using an exfoliating cream or gel once or twice a week clear away those dead skin cells to leave your skin cleaner, brighter and fresher.

Splash warm water over your face and dab the exfoliator cream on your forehead, nose, cheeks and chin and then begin slowly massaging it around your face using small circular movements. This is perfect for boosting the circulation, but avoid the delicate areas around the eyes. Don't forget the neck. Rinse off with lots of warm water and then finally a splash of cold water. Pat your skin dry with a soft towel and apply a moisturiser.

Get Fit: Days 1–7

Okay it's here; you've done all your preparation, and you know what the next 28 days will involve. The best and most effective way to undertake the programme is to start on a positive note and preferably on a Friday, thus giving you the weekend to get into some sort of routine.

Whether you are a working woman or a busy mum at home, the next 28 days may mark the biggest changes you are ever going to make in your life so be prepared. Make up a chart (see page 127) and stick it on your kitchen wall so that you remember what you must include each day in your programme.

It's important to keep a diary in which you can record your day's plan, what you ate, how you took time out for yourself, and then at the end of each day make a note of how you felt. Obviously some days you will find more to write about than others, but keeping this and then referring to it when you have negative days will keep you motivated. Weigh yourself today only!

Here is a typical plan for day one, but naturally times will differ and the order in which activities are done may also change according to your lifestyle.

7.30am Glass of hot water and squeeze of lemon juice.
7.45am Early morning shower
8.15am Breakfast. On the first day choose something you are familiar with, such as cereal, to ease you gently into the programme.

9.15am After clearing away the breakfast dishes, begin day one with a gentle body workout but take it easy and don't over exert yourself.
10.15am Sit down and relax with a glass of water and don't think too hard about those parts of your body that may be aching at the moment. The next time will be better. Whilst you are sitting, why not practise 20 minutes of hibernation to give your body time to settle down.
11.00am Although you are on the programme, don't forget there is always the housework to do and in fact if you put sufficient energy into doing the this you will be burning up even more calories.
1.00pm Time for lunch. For a healthy sandwich, take two medium slices of wholemeal bread and fill with low-fat spread, a small can of tuna in brine, a few lettuce leaves, a small tomato and several slices of cucumber. Finish off with a banana.
3.00pm Go out for at least a 30-minute brisk walk. You'll tone up your legs and buttocks and, if you take long strides, your lower tummy muscles will benefit too. Set yourself a goal and see if you can achieve it.
4.00pm Make yourself a cold drink of freshly squeezed

range juice to revive you after that long walk. Why not take the opportunity to make this your creative part of the day when you can dedicate it to doing something artistic – paint a picture, write a poem or take up tapestry or embroidery.

.00pm Time to think about dinner – why not prepare chicken salad, taking advantage of the variety of salad vegetables around. And if still peckish afterwards, have some fruit.

.00pm Have an early bath. Add some salts into it and relax for a while.

.00pm Snuggle into your dressing gown and before going to bed, spend some time thinking calm thoughts to relax your mind and prepare you for a good night's sleep.

Don't forget – as you complete each activity tick it off on your chart and before you go to sleep remember to record in your diary how you felt, both the good and bad points. Plan what you intend doing the next day.

Remainder of the week

The remainder of week one should follow more or less the same basic routine, but adding in different foods and trying different exercises

Measurements chart

As you change your routine to include more exercise and reform your eating habits, you will find that not only will you have toned up the muscles all over your body to give you a slimmer look, but you will feel generally a lot healthier and have lots more energy!

You can record your measurements each week using this simple chart.

It's a good idea to keep an exercise diary to record your increased stamina and fitness. For example:

Date	Exercise	Repetitions	Comments
01.04	Crunches	20	Agony!
	Hips/Buttocks	30 each	Breathless
02.04	Stomach	20	Exhausted
	Swimming	30 mins	Tired but feel great
03.04	Hips/Buttocks	40 each	Much better today
	Stomach	30	Puffed – easier today
	Walking	2 miles	Brisk and energizing
04.04	Crunches	30	Getting much easier

	Week 1	Week 2	Week 3	Week 4
Date				
Weight				
Bust				
Waist				
Hips				

Get Fit: Days 8–14

You will by now have established a routine and perhaps made some changes.

So are you ready for week two?

7.30am Glass of hot water and squeeze of lime juice.

7.45am Early morning shower.

8.15am Breakfast. Have a change in your second week – why not try a poached egg on wholemeal toast.

9.15am By now you should have extended your target for walking and so be able to walk a little further.

10.15am After the walk your feet may feel a little tender so why not treat them to some pampering that will help make them feel nice and smooth. See the recipe for Foot Mask, below.

11.00am Make this your creative time and carry on with the picture you were painting or the tapestry you began and to make it more relaxing play some music in the background.

1.00pm Time for lunch. Often the worst time of the day as you try to think up tasty meals. This is why it's a good idea to work out a week in advance what you intend eating and stick to those meals. Write them up as a daily menu and pin it in the kitchen. Today why not have a baked jacket potato filled with a small can of mixed chilli beans and served with a green salad.

3.00pm Do a total workout routine.

4.00pm Spend time exfoliating the skin

6.00pm Time to prepare dinner. How about Chicken Risotto and finish with a banana for dessert.

7.00pm Go into a quiet room and spend some time hibernating to help clear your mind of all tensions and frustrations. Just being alone for 20 minutes can help to revitalize and rejuvenate the body.

8.00pm Treat yourself to a relaxing bath and give those muscles a long, lingering soak by adding a few drops of sweet marjoram, ginger or black pepper oil to the bathwater.

Don't forget – as you complete each activity tick it off on your chart and before you go to sleep remember to record in your diary how you felt, both the good and bad points. Plan what you intend doing the next day.

Remainder of the week

Just continue keeping to more or less the same routine you have already established but add in different foods and try out different exercises. Pamper yourself with a salt bath.

Foot Mask
2 bananas
2 teaspoons olive oil
2 tablespoons fine sea salt
Juice of half a lemon

Mash the bananas in a bowl, then add the rest of the ingredients. Mix them thoroughly. Place the feet on a towel and massage the mixture into them. Leave it on for about 10 minutes and then wash off using warm water. Afterwards apply lots of moisturiser.

Get Fit: Days 15–21

You are now beginning the second half of your programme and into the
third week already.

There may be times you become bored with doing the exercises or toning up routine, but you are doing it for a good reason so just keep on and reap the rewards in another week!

7.30am Glass of hot water with a squeeze of lemon or lime juice.

7.45am Morning shower.

8.15am Breakfast. A bowl of muesli with a handful of dried apricots and bananas and some skimmed milk. A cup of herbal tea.

9.15am Try to do the full workout – by now you should be able to do far more of each routine. Look in your diary to check on your progress.

10.15am Arrange to meet up with an old friend and leave the house earlier so you can go for a walk beforehand. If you feel you are in need of some support with your workout routine, why not call in to your local gym and check whether they have any classes you could join.

12.00pm Have lunch with a friend. Perhaps choose a chicken salad and a glass of iced water.

2.15pm Back at home it's time for a little rest and hibernation.

3.00pm Do some housework or perhaps some gardening. The grass needs mowing and some plants need pruning, and there is also weeding to be done.

4.15pm Time for a glass of unsweetened orange juice and an hour of creative inspiration.

6.00pm Prepare dinner – Chicken Celebration tonight.

7.00pm As a treat, bake a Ginger and Carrot Cake.

8.00pm Have a salt bath, then an early night. Record what happened during the day and plan the following week's menus.

Don't forget – as you complete each activity tick it off on your chart and before you go to sleep remember to record in your diary how you felt, both the good and bad points. Plan what you intend doing the next day. Why don't you take some photographs of yourself midway through the programme just to see what you looked like at different stages.

Remainder of the week

By now you will have established a pattern of exercising and also the creative hour to spend however you wish. You can always alternate and change things around, you may even find that you want to replace walking with something entirely different. The number one priority is that you stick to the programme.

Get Fit: Days 22–28

You are on the last lap. This is the final week and you have come a long way so there is n
turning back now. The end is actually in sight.

Once you hit the age of 30-40 you've got to be careful about activities that involve pounding. Running takes its toll on the joints but swimming improves the metabolism and cardiovascular fitness; tones you from head to toe and it's also a great calorie burning activity. Start with 20 minutes and if you can do five lengths of the pool, next time see if you can do six lengths, gradually building it up.

7.30am Have a glass of hot water with a squeeze of lemon juice.
9.15am Instead of doing your usual exercise i.e. walking or cycling, why not go for a swim at your local pool. An invigorating early morning swim is healthy and refreshing and it sets you up for the rest of the day.
10.15am Breakfast. A wedge of melon served with 115g (4oz) grapes and a small carton of low-fat yogurt.
11.00am Swimming can be refreshing but also tiring so give yourself a little time and do some relaxation.
1.00pm Lunchtime. How about a Spanish Omelette.
2.00pm Creative hour
3.30pm You should by now have increased the length of your workout sessions so prepare yourself and start pumping those muscles.
5.00pm Have a cool glass of water with a slice of lemon and sit down to think over your month's busy schedule and what you have achieved, what you would like to have achieved and feel very proud of what you have done
7.00pm Go out for a celebration meal. Whatever

restaurant you go to, choose your menu wisely – you don't want all that good work going to waste.

Now is the time to weigh yourself and take your measurements, then look back at the beginning of th chart to see the amount of weight you have lost.

Here are some suggestions for meals that won't ruin all your good work:
If eating French
- Crudités with garlic dip (raw sliced vegetables)
- Moules Marinières (mussels cooked in shallots, lemon, herbs and white wine)
- Steak au Poivre (steak with a peppered sauce)

If eating Italian
- Minestrone soup (made with white beans, peas, onion, ham, celery, herbs, garlic, pasta and white wine)
- Spaghetti Napoli (pasta with a low-fat tomato sauce)

If eating Greek
- Spanokopitta (pastries stuffed with feta cheese and spinach)
- Souvlaki (pieces of meat marinated in olive oil and lemon juice then grilled on skewers)
- Greek Salad (sliced tomatoes, onion, black olives and lettuce with feta cheese)

If eating Spanish
- Gazpacho (cold soup with red peppers, onions, tomatoes, cucumber soaked in oil, garlic and vinegar)
- Arroz alla Alicantina (rice with chicken)

Activity Record Chart

Record your activities every day using this table

DAILY ACTIVITIES	1	2	3	4	5	6	7	8	9	10	11	12	13	14	15	16	17	18	19	20	21	22	23	24	25	26	27	28
Glass of hot water and lemon or lime juice																												
Daily energy shower																												
Breakfast																												
Lunch																												
Dinner																												
1.75 litres (3 pints) water																												
Wide variety of fresh fruit																												
Wide variety of fresh vegetables																												
30 mins walk																												
30 mins exercise																												
20 mins hibernation																												
Epsom salts bath every 3 days																												
Salt scrub once a week																												
Only moderate use of salt																												

Congratulations!

You've done it – you've completed the 28-day Get Fit for Summer programme successfully

But old habits are hard to break and just as there have been moments in the last 28 days when you felt unable to go on, there are sure to be days in the future when you feel like going back to your old ways and not thinking about what you are eating. When you get moments like those, read back through your diary to remind yourself how you coped with those down days. Look through the photographs you had taken at different stages of your programme and glean from them the confidence to continue.

And it is worth remembering that different stages of life can create their own problems:

In Your Twenties – welcome the office bum.
This is when many of us end up sitting at a desk for 6-7 hours a day. Unfortunately it is also the time when the mind is stimulated but not the buttocks, so make sure they don't turn flabby. You need to integrate some cardiovascular exercising, especially those directed towards the gluteal region, i.e. step classes, brisk walking, skipping and running.

In Your Thirties – welcome the baby belly.
A time in life when many women have their children, resulting in flabby stomach muscles that need a little more than breathing in. If you don't work on this area the muscles will just remain lazy and flabby. Remember to ask your doctor's advice if you have recently had a baby.

In Your Forties – welcome sagging arm muscles.
This is the time when muscles in the backs of the arms may begin to follow gravity. To counteract this problem and tone up the muscles, it is important to start exercising the shoulders and arms.

In Your Fifties – welcome thunder thighs.
Although active when younger, with the passing of years motivating one's legs to go for a long walk can get harder but any type of cardiovascular training will remedy this. Try dancing, brisk walking or you're never too old to take up cycling.

Achieving and maintaining a healthy weight requires a lifelong commitment to healthy eating. The three most important lessons you should have learnt from your programme are to:
✓ Eat a balanced healthy diet
✓ Eat three meals a day
✓ Take some daily exercise

The 28 Day Plan

FLAT STOMACH

You Can Have a Flat Stomach

Have you striven for years to attain a well-toned lean stomach; have you tried every diet imaginable; stuck rigidly to a daily ritual of sit-ups and even contemplated spending your savings on liposuction, all for the sake of having a flat stomach?

Forget all that and enrol yourself on this 28-day programme which will guarantee you trim and well-toned abdominal muscles and a stomach to be proud of. And with the money you have saved by not choosing liposuction, treat yourself to a new outfit to show off your flat stomach.

Reasons for a flabby stomach

Why is it that some people who have never eaten a crispbread in their life, never ventured into a gym, and for whom 'healthy' eating is a dirty word still have washboard-like stomachs to die for? Is genetics to blame, the after-effects of childbirth, bad eating habits, a sedentary lifestyle, even bad posture? All are possibilities but there are also several other reasons including:

- Age
- Beer belly
- Lack of exercise
- Motherhood
- Stress
- The monthly cycle
- Trapped wind

Lack of exercise

If you plan to follow this 28-day programme, you must give up feeble excuses such as you haven't time,

you are too busy or that you have something better to do – the only way to deal with excess flab around the middle is a combined programme of exercise and healthy eating.

Extra flesh gained around the abdominal area is difficult to move because, once those fat cells have formed, although they may shrink in size they are constantly lying in wait, ready to pounce in response to a moment's lapse. If you don't work the muscles, they will turn flabby, but once they are regularly exercised, toned and strengthened, they respond in no time at all.

Your age

It is a pity that so much attention nowadays is focused upon the way a woman looks and the changes caused by ageing, especially when you are over 30.

In truth this is the age when a woman's metabolism naturally slows down, because the body has reached a turning point when nature is equipping it with extra baggage, generally in the shape of excess flesh around the waist, thighs and upper arms. The only remedy is to accept these changes gracefully, but at the same time to fight back.

By all means enjoy the occasional cream cake but make sure it is just 'occasional'. Experts recommend that the only way to keep your shape in trim is to reduce your intake of calories and to increase the amount of exercise you take. And that's what this 28-day programme is all about.

Bloating

The 'time of the month' plays havoc not only with emotions but also body shape, sometimes making you feel that you look like a beached whale! The hormone progesterone is the guilty party. Generally a week before the onset of your period, the body begins to produce extra progesterone (the hormone responsible for causing fluid retention) in preparation for an egg to be fertilized. Naturally this fluid manifests itself around the stomach. Once the 'all-clear' signal is heard and the body knows that it is not pregnant, progesterone levels drop to their normal level, excess fluid is released through your urine, and the stomach returns to its normal shape.

It is during this difficult build-up period that your mind often plays tricks on you. The raised levels of progesterone can affect one's mood and body image, so although rationally you know you aren't any fatter, you still feel that you are.

Trapped wind

The body is an amazing organism but there are times when it refuses to accept quietly the foods it is being fed and reacts in unpredictable ways. Many find complex sugar foods, such as fruit, vegetables and beans, are difficult to digest and the result is intestinal gas that can give the stomach a rather bloated appearance and an uncomfortable feeling of fullness.

The most effective way to deal with this is to monitor your diet and eliminate those foods which are responsible.

Stress

Whenever you are worried or under stress, the body reacts. Some people find that the stomach is particularly affected when it is suddenly bombarded with large amounts of the stress hormone cortisol.

Because the stomach area has more receptors than any other part of the body, the hormone is automatically pumped into the fat cells lying around the waist where it settles.

In order to deal with stress and to reduce the effect it has on your stomach, there are several positive things you can do:

- Learn to relax
- Take regular exercise
- Practise deep breathing
- Have a good laugh
- If you drink or smoke, cut down

Beer Belly

Beer is not the only culprit; in fact any alcoholic drink can increase the size of the stomach simply because every gram of alcohol contains seven calories, almost twice as many per gram of most other carbohydrates or protein. So if you know that alcohol is the cause of your flabby stomach, there is only one answer: give up drinking the stuff!

Why toned muscles look so much better

Looking good and feeling good go hand in hand and the fact that you are conscious of your flabby stomach muscles will do little to boost your self-confidence and make you feel good about yourself. So time invested in dealing with the problem will change your whole outlook on life:

✓ You will look good in whatever clothes you wear
✓ Your confidence in yourself will soar
✓ Your posture will be improved
✓ You will not suffer back discomfort

By the end of the 28 days

If you have decided to undertake this programme, rest assured that you will not regret it. Just don't become too obsessive about what you eat, or about the amount of exercise you try to do. Set yourself realistic targets, ones that you know you can achieve. Make up a chart and monitor your daily progress, marking down how many sit-ups or stomach exercises you managed on a particular day and then try increasing them the following day, but do it gradually. Keep reminding yourself why you are doing it.

Read these six motivational sentences each time you feel your willpower sagging:

I will keep focused, and by the end of these 28 days I will:

- **Feel healthier**
- **Feel more confident**
- **Feel much better about how I look in snug-fitting clothes**
- **Will want to wear short cropped tops**
- **Will not have a bad back**
- **My posture will be improved**

By the end of the programme, with perseverance and dedication, you will have achieved every one of them.

No more excuses about starting tomorrow or next week, there is no time like today! So start planning now and let's get working towards your dream of achieving perfect flat abs.

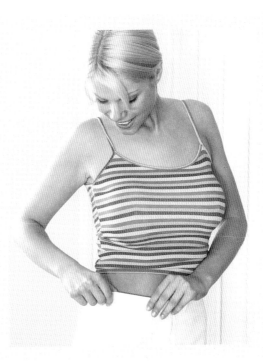

Learning To Exercise

A large part of this programme deals with exercise and in particular how to tone the
abdominal muscles that work in conjunction with the back muscles to help maintain good posture.
But sometimes all the hard work can come to nothing because it is not fully understood how the
abdominal muscles work.

Stomach muscles

Before you start to exercise your abdominal muscles,
it is important to understand how they work.

Basically the stomach area is made up of four main
abdominal muscles:

Internal and external obliques

Two diagonal lengths of muscle
called the external and internal
obliques run across the front of
the ribs and around to the
spine. Their primary function is
to help the torso when twisting,
bending from side to side and
also to maintain its stability

Tranversus abdominis (deep)

Running horizontally from the
lower ribs to the spine, this
group of muscles hold and
maintain the shape of the
organs within the abdomen.
Each time we hold our tummies
in, these are the muscles which
are working.

Rectus abdominis (front)

A muscle that runs vertically from the sternum to the
pubic bone – its main role is to help move the torso
from a lying position to an upright one. Problems
occur as weight is put on around the midsection and

the muscles are engulfed beneath it and become
unable to retain their former defined shape.

As more weight settles, then it doesn't matter if
you wear a girdle or hold your stomach in all day, it
will not make any difference. The fat is there to stay
unless you decide to do
something about it – and that
means exercise. Without regular
exercise, the muscles will begin
to weaken and you will find
yourself with a flabby stomach.

When to exercise

Many experts recommend
exercising first thing in the
morning but it really depends on
individual preference.

If, for example, you are in
full-time employment, you may
find yourself having to exercise
in the morning or evening,
either before you leave for work
or after you return home. If you
have young children, you may
well choose to exercise when they are at school or
playgroup. The most important thing is to choose a
time which is convenient for you and with which you
feel comfortable.

How to begin exercising

Providing you are under 35 and in good health, there is little reason to see a doctor before embarking on an exercise programme. However, if you have recently given birth or been inactive for several years, then you should, for your own safety, consider making an appointment to see your doctor first.

If you suffer from any of these medical conditions, you should definitely seek medical advice:

- Arthritis or other bone problems
- Extreme breathlessness after mild exertion
- Family history of early stroke or heart attacks
- Frequent dizzy spells
- Heart trouble
- High blood pressure
- Other known or suspected disease
- Severe muscular, ligament or tendon problems

Basic warm-up movements

Loosening up the body before exercising is important because it prepares the muscles and joints for the workout and also increases the heart rate causing the blood to pump faster around the body. Consequently the harder the muscles work, the more beneficial the exercise will be. There are lots of warm-up exercises to choose from but basically they should be a blend of rhythmic stretching so that all parts of the body are limbered up and ready to go.

Shoulders To loosen up tense shoulder and neck

muscles, stand with your feet slightly apart, then roll the left shoulder backwards ten times. Repeat with the right shoulder, at the same time shifting your weight from the left foot to the right foot.

Arms and knees This is a great one for overall posture. Stand up straight, tummy tucked in, then swing both arms up and then swing them down, bending the knees as you bring the arms down in a gentle smooth action. Repeat 15 times.

Side to side With your feet evenly spaced apart, knees gently bent and hands firmly on the hips, very slowly lean over to one side stretching the arm out at the same time as far as you can. Return to a standing position and stretch to the other side. Repeat four stretches on each side.

Waisting time This is good for the spine and waist. With your feet slightly parted, knees gently bent, hips facing forward, raise the arms nearly to shoulder level and, taking it easy, twist the body from side to side. Do four twists each side.

Stretching Sitting on the floor cross-legged, place one hand slightly behind you, then bring the other arm up and, with the palm facing outward, stretch up as far as you are able. Hold for the count of ten, bring the arm back down and repeat with the other arm.

Body stretch This is a pleasant exercise. Simply lie on your back and stretch your arms and legs as far as possible. Hold for five seconds and then relax.

Types of Exercise

There are two main types of exercise that will help you to attain a flat stomach. One is aerobic exercise and the other is toning or strengthening work. Both are important.

Aerobic exercises

These exercises help to burn fat and involve any form of activity that makes you feel a little out of breath. They include:

- Cycling
- Jogging
- Power walking
- Running
- Skipping
- Swimming

Toning or strengthening exercises

These exercises build up specific muscle groups and, in doing so, increase the rate at which calories are used up.

Some exercises to try

There are many different toning and strengthening exercises which are perfect for getting to work on the abdominals. Ideally you should try doing each of these exercises slowly and carefully, concentrating on the areas of the body on which you are working. Start by doing 5-10 minutes each day, and aim to build up to about 20. You will find a workout mat very useful for the floor exercises.

Crunch

The basic exercise for strengthening and toning the upper abdominals.

1. Lie with your back flat on the floor, knees bent and feet spaced shoulder-width apart.

2. Place your hands behind your ears but do not hold on to your head or neck.

3. Now for the difficult part. Keeping your eyes focused directly on the ceiling and your elbows wide apart, slowly raise your shoulders off the ground, pulling in the stomach muscles as you do so. Do not try to raise more than your shoulders off the floor.

4. Then slowly lower the shoulders back to the floor, remembering to exhale as you come up and inhale as you lower down again.

5. At this stage don't push yourself and risk putting undue strain on your back. It isn't the quantity of crunches that matters, it's the quality.

Ready to crunch

Here is a handy tip if you find tummy crunches rather difficult: spend 3 minutes lying flat on your back pressing your spine into the floor and holding your tummy muscles tight for a count of ten. Twenty a day should enable you to progress to trying a few crunches after a few days.

Full sit-ups

1. Lie on the floor in the same position as for the crunch with your hands gently resting behind your ears.

2. Now pull your whole body up as far as you can, remembering to exhale as you rise up and keeping your feet flat on the ground. The aim is to sit upright, but very few people manage this in the beginning, so don't worry too much if you cannot do it. Just go as far as you can without feeling any undue strain on your back.

3. Slowly roll back down to the floor, remembering to inhale.

4. Then relax for a moment, gather your energy and have another try.

Isometric abdominal curl

An ideal exercise for strengthening all the abdominal muscles.

1. Lie flat on your back, hands gently placed behind the ears.

2. Place your feet flat on the floor, with the heels pulled up close to your buttocks.

3. Tighten your abdominal muscles and at the same time push your lower back down into the floor.

4. With your back now firmly on the ground, lift your feet just a couple of inches up off the floor, hold for ten seconds.

5. Then slowly release, rest and repeat.

Cooling down

Just as you need to prepare the body for exercising with warming-up exercises, you also need to cool it down after you have finished. After all, your body has been through quite an ordeal! You will find lots of different warming-up and cooling-down exercises in various books but here are a few of my favourites for you to try.

Tips for sit-ups

As with most forms of exercise it is important to get the maximum benefit out of each. Many people fail to do sit-ups correctly so here are a few important pointers:

- Keep your head in line with your spine
- As you breathe out, press your tongue against the roof of your mouth to prevent yourself from over-tightening the jaw and neck muscles
- To prevent straining your neck when rising, don't focus your gaze on your knees; instead focus on something in the distance
- Don't lace your fingers behind your neck when rising; the temptation to pull on the neck for support is hard to resist, instead, use your elbows for balance

Spine relaxer

Sitting cross-legged, tummy held in, bend forward and hold your arms out on the floor in front of you. Hold for the count of ten and then relax.

Back and arms

This may sound rather tricky but it is very relaxing. Again sitting cross-legged on the floor with your back straight, clench your hands behind your back, clasp your fingers together and gently pull on them for a count of ten. Then relax.

Tummy tenser

Lie face down on the floor, with your elbows slightly bent so that they are under your shoulders. Making sure the forearms and elbows remain on the floor, raise both head and shoulders very slowly. Hold this position for a count of six, then relax.

Exercising Options

If the concept of donning a leotard and taking up step aerobics at the local gym fills you with horror, or the mere mention of jogging causes an outbreak of athlete's foot, relax – there are plenty of other options! We shall look at some of them on these two pages.

Kick boxing

This activity has become very popular with both men and women. Furthermore it:

✓ Helps lower body fat by toning the muscles
✓ Helps people to work out their stresses and frustrations
✓ Improves power, balance and overall agility
✓ Increases muscular endurance and strength
✓ Many women say that it enhances their self-confidence
✓ Tones and conditions the upper part of the body

Many local gyms run kick-boxing classes, so why not check them out?

Cycling

The idea of squeezing into a pair of Lycra shorts and hitting the highways on your bike may not fill you with an adrenalin rush but when you consider its health benefits, it is well-worth a second thought.

Cycling is an ideal exercise for toning up muscles getting out in the fresh air and just popping out to the shops. If you are a little hesitant of what people may say, you could always borrow or hire an indoor cycle or nip along to your local gym to use their

cycling machines. Admittedly, cycling indoors can be a little boring, although you can always wear some earphones and tune in to some music to while away the time spent exercising.

Water aerobics

This is based on normal aerobic exercises, i.e. running, jogging and walking, but instead of it being done on land, the exercises are performed in water, generally at a local swimming pool. It is a perfect form of all-round exercise and, as your confidence grows, so you will find yourself able to move into a deeper section

Take care
If you have any chronic medical conditions or back problems, you should consult your doctor before starting any exercise programme.

of the pool. Essentially the idea is to work the muscles against the resistance of the water while maintaining an upright stance throughout the exercise sequence. It is a great way of burning up calories efficiently.

Power walking

How about taking up power walking? Not a gentle saunter around the park but a brisk walk, head and shoulders back, arms swinging, tummy held in and taking long determined strides. Not only will it encourage better posture, but power walking is also ideal for toning up the thighs, arms and legs. The more intense you make it, the more calories you will burn up. And when you are powering along, make sure that you take in deep breaths of fresh air.

Gardening

If you don't feel like doing anything beyond your home patch and you have a garden, then look no further for your daily exercise. Mow the lawn – it's great for toning up the abdominal muscles; how about pruning those high branches – no better exercise for toning the arms and back; or pull up weeds – it is the ideal answer for working on those thighs as you bend and straighten. It also helps to tone up buttocks and arms, and the bonus is that your garden looks good too.

Exercising for new mothers

After giving birth, some women are sometimes devastated to find themselves left with saggy stomach muscles. While other parts of the body slowly get back into shape, the stomach often seems reluctant to return to its former shape. But don't worry – with some gentle exercising, those over-stretched muscles will soon disappear and you will be able to climb into those clinging denims again. But before you put on your training clothes and set yourself an exhausting

schedule to follow, here are a few important rules:

• Check with your doctor or local health visitor about exercising and ask if they have any gentle firming-up exercises that they can recommend. Remember childbirth is a traumatic experience for the body and you cannot expect it to snap back into its previous condition just like that.

• Develop a routine. Wait until the baby is having a nap, or has gone to bed, before you start exercising.

• Make sure that each of your movements is slow and take adequate rest breaks between exercises.

• Warm up and cool down before and after each exercise session by doing a few gentle stretching movements.

• If one day you feel under the weather or it is hot, reduce your routine by half, and make sure that you drink plenty of water to prevent dehydration.

• Simply taking the baby out for a walk is good exercise; remember that a happy contented mother makes for a happy contented baby.

A Good Diet

If you turn green with envy every time you see a young model flaunting her well-toned abdomen,

don't imagine that she didn't have to make an effort to achieve it.

Remember, it doesn't matter how much exercise you do, it can never fully compensate for poor eating habits. The only way to eliminate surplus fat is:

✓ To change your eating habits
✓ To increase your level of exercise

By sticking to these two basic rules, you will be well on your way to achieving that perfect stomach.

Nourishing the body

Changing eating habits does not mean that you have to follow a diet and count all your calories. What it does mean is that you should eat healthy nourishing

food containing a balance of essential nutrients, which in turn are derived from the following:

Carbohydrates: These provide energy for the body and come in two basic forms. Simple carbohydrates basically comprise sugar and very little else. Complex carbohydrates include starchy foods, such as bread, potatoes, cereal, pasta, rice, etc.

Fats: The number one enemy in terms of a lean body but essential for helping to insulate and protect the organs and nerves. It is found in varying quantities in numerous foods such as butter, cheese, lard, snack-type foods, fatty meat, etc. The basic principle of a healthy diet is to reduce the amount of fat you eat and stick to a low-fat diet. It doesn't mean cutting fat out totally, but rather choosing those foods sensibly and checking on the label for a low-fat alternative.

Proteins: The body breaks down the protein from food into its component parts, called amino acids, which it then uses to build and repair tissue and muscle. Protein is found in foods such as meat, poultry, fish, dairy foods, eggs, beans, lentils and nuts, cheese, yogurt, etc.

Minerals: These are vital to the human body as they help to form bones, strengthen teeth, maintain a healthy immune system and support the vitamins in their work. Calcium, for instance, is important for helping to build strong bones and teeth.

Vitamins: These substances are vital for good health and the maintenance of various bodily functions. A well-balanced diet containing plenty of fresh foods should be rich in vitamins. .

Each day on the programme make sure that you:

Eat three meals a day: breakfast, lunch and dinner. Your daily intake should include:

- 170g (6oz) protein food – fish, poultry, cottage cheese, lean meat
- 340g (12oz) vegetables
- 340g (12oz) fresh fruit
- 170g (6oz) bread, cereal, potatoes, rice, pasta
- 450ml (3/4 pint) skimmed/semi-skimmed milk
- 150ml (1/4 pint) unsweetened orange, grapefruit or apple juice
- Tea and coffee can be drunk using milk from your quota but try drinking more water instead

Foods that can cause problems

Some people react badly to certain foods that cause bloatedness, gas and other related digestive disorders. Often it is possible to trace those foods responsible by trial and error and so eliminate them from your diet.

If you suffer from bloatedness, it may well be triggered off by eating one of the foods listed below. If you are unsure, keep a record every time you eat them to monitor whether there are any recurrent symptoms and you can avoid the food in question.

- Alcohol
- Beans
- Bran
- Brussels sprouts
- Cauliflower
- Cheese
- Coffee
- Fizzy drinks
- Garlic
- Onion
- Peas
- Processed foods, i.e. canned meats
- Pulses
- Salt
- Tea

On the other hand, certain foods can counteract that bloatedness, especially when it is related to pre-menstrual syndrome (PMS).

- Celery
- Citrus fruits
- Fish
- Green leafy vegetables
- Meat
- Natural water
- Parsley
- Wholegrains

Ban these foods!

If you are really serious about following this programme then certain types of food must be banned, unless in very special circumstances they are unavoidable:

Meats

- Black pudding
- Fat or skin from all meat and poultry
- Goose and other fatty meat
- Haggis
- Pâté
- Pork pie
- Salami
- Sausage
- Scotch eggs

Dairy produce

- All cheese, except cottage cheese
- Butter
- Cream
- Dripping
- Egg custard
- Eggs and other related products
- Full-fat milk
- Ice cream
- Lard
- Low-fat spreads containing more than 4 per cent fat and all similar products
- Margarine
- Quiches
- Suet

Other foods

- All fried foods
- Avocados
- Biscuits
- Cakes
- Chocolate
- Chocolate spread
- Cocoa and related products
- Crisps
- Fudge
- Lemon curd
- Marzipan
- Pastries – sweet and savoury
- Peanut butter
- Sauces and dressings which contain cream, whole milk or eggs
- Sponge puddings
- Sweets
- Toffees

Low-fat food

While you are on this 28-day programme, you will have to cut out certain favourite foods, but with such a wide and varied choice remaining for you, that will not seem such a hardship unless you are a veritable slave to cakes and chocolate. All the time you are abstaining, remember the reason that you doing so – a lean, taut abdomen.

There are several ways to help cut back the fat content in your food:

1. When shopping, make sure that you always pay attention to the nutritional contents printed on the side of the packaged food you buy. The two most important details are the total fat and energy content. The energy value on the sides of food packaging will be shown in kilojoules or kilocalories (kcal). The kcal figure tells you the number of calories per 100 grams (4oz). Ideally select foods containing no more than 4g (0.14oz) of fat per 100 grams of weight. Don't be tempted by those foods that simply say they are low-fat – always check the label to confirm this for yourself.

. Use semi-skimmed or skimmed milk.

. Whenever possible, steam, grill or bake food, instead of frying it.

. Use low-fat yogurt instead of cream, ice cream or vaporated milk.

. Eat cottage cheese instead of full-fat cheese.

. Add more fish and poultry to your diet.

. Always trim any visible fat off meat.

. Simmer ingredients in vegetable stock instead of shallow frying them in lard or butter.

Of course you do need a small amount of fat in your diet but, by following these guidelines, you will ensure that you do not get too much.

What you can have

It's not all bad news as there are lots of tempting and tasty foods that you can enjoy throughout the programme and lots of delicious menus you can experiment with. For example:

Bread: The staff of life and fine to eat providing it is wholemeal.

Cottage cheese: You don't have to stick with the plain variety, there are lots of differently flavoured low-fat ones that make a refreshing addition to a salad. Try some spread on crispbread for a quick lunchtime snack or, if you are having friends around, add a handful of herbs and garlic to plain cottage cheese as it makes a tasty dip .

Gravy: If you cannot face a meal without gravy, just ensure that you make it using gravy powder and not the meat juices.

Pasta and rice: Nutritious and satisfying – whenever possible stick to the wholemeal varieties.

Vegetables: You can choose whatever you like, even potatoes, but just make sure they are steamed or boiled rather than fried and don't add butter! Eaten raw, carrots, celery and pea pods are all very tasty.

Sauces: To add some extra flavour to a slice of bread or to a salad, to pour over fish or pep up a pasta dish, you can have a virtually free range with the following:

- Brown, chilli, horseradish, mint, Worcester sauces
- Fat-free salad dressings
- Lemon juice
- Marmite
- Mustard
- Oil-free vinaigrette dressing
- Soy sauce
- Vinegar

Drinks: Aim to drink at least five or six large glasses of water each day, especially during the summer months. Tea and coffee are fine providing any milk is deducted from your daily quota and, if possible, try drinking it without adding sugar. It's far healthier. Diet drinks are fine, but natural water is even better and the occasional weekend glass of wine is allowed.

A New Eating Regime

The main principle to remember when following this eating plan is that you must maximize your fat loss by adopting a low-fat diet and taking plenty of exercise.

The main reason why people don't succeed when following an eating regime is that they:
- are impatient and expect to see results immediately
- are not sufficiently motivated
- don't eat enough at the prescribed mealtimes
- don't understand their bodies' needs
- eat too little overall
- exercise on an empty stomach

Here are some suggestions for you to select from – there is lots of variety. To make it easier why not decide every day on the meals for the following day and, whenever possible, prepare them before going to bed. In that way you will not have to worry about what to eat as soon as you get up.

Breakfast suggestions

Each of the following may be served with some of the milk from the daily allowance:
- 25g (1oz) muesli, 1 teaspoon sugar, 1 sliced banana
- 50g (2oz) All-Bran with 1 teaspoon sugar, 1 chopped apple
- 50g (2oz) cornflakes with 1 teaspoon sugar, 110g (4oz) strawberries
- 2 Weetabix with 1 teaspoon sugar, 1 sliced banana
- To make your own muesli, place 15g (½oz) porridge oats, 6 sultanas, 1 teaspoon clear honey, 75ml (3fl oz) skimmed milk and 150ml (5fl oz) natural yogurt in a bowl, cover and place it in the refrigerator to chill until morning.

Fruity breakfasts
- 1 grapefruit and 2 small pots of low-fat yogurt
- 200g (7oz) stewed fruit cooked without sugar and topped with 1 small carton of low-fat yogurt
- 300g (11oz) can grapefruit segments in natural juice
- 5 canned prunes in natural juice and 1 small low-fat natural yogurt
- Slice of melon topped with 110g (4oz) grapes and 1 small low-fat yogurt
- Chop up one apple, peel and slice a banana and an orange, then mix them together with a handful of grapes in a bowl.

Hot options
- 2 slices wholemeal bread topped with 3 teaspoons marmalade or honey
- 1 whole muffin and 1 apple
- 1 small poached egg served on 1 slice wholemeal toast spread with Marmite and ½ fresh grapefruit

Lunchtime ideas

If midday is a hectic time for you, slow down and take stock. Have a salad one day, a jacket potato with a favourite topping the next, a sandwich the following day and keep ringing the changes to add variety to your midday meal.
- For an apple and carrot salad, sprinkle the juice of half a lemon juice over 3 sliced apples to prevent them discolouring. Mix 450g (1lb) of grated carrots, 3 tablespoons raisins, 1 tablespoon sunflower seeds and 2 tablespoons cashew nuts in the juice with the apples. Tear half an iceberg lettuce into strips and put in a bowl, add the carrot and apple mixture and then blend into the vinaigrette dressing (recipe follows).

For an oil-free vinaigrette, mix 3 tablespoons white wine vinegar, 1 tablespoon lemon juice, 1$^{1}/_{2}$ teaspoons black pepper, $^{1}/_{2}$ teaspoon salt, 1 teaspoon sugar, $^{1}/_{2}$ teaspoon French mustard and a handful of chopped assorted herbs together. Taste and add more salt or sugar as required. The dressing will keep in the refrigerator for up to three days.

For a tasty raw beetroot salad, mix together 2 sticks finely chopped celery, 225g (8oz) peeled and grated raw beetroot and 2 large dessert apples, cored and chopped and grated carrot to taste. Add enough oil-free vinaigrette dressing to moisten the salad.

Rice salad is great at lunchtime. Chop up a chunk of cucumber, a tomato and a green pepper very finely. Put them into a bowl. Add 50g (2oz) boiled brown rice, 25g (1oz) cooked sweetcorn and 25g (1oz) cooked peas. Finally add a dash of soy sauce, a sprinkling of black pepper and a pinch of salt.

This recipe for stuffed tomatoes serves two. Using a sharp knife cut off the tops of 2 large, firm tomatoes and scoop out the seeds. Open and drain the juice from a small can of sweetcorn and the brine from a small can of tuna fish before transferring them into a bowl. Add 2 tablespoons low-calorie mayonnaise, stir the mixture and spoon it back into the tomatoes.

Dinner suggestions

Fish is easily digestible, nutritious and very versatile. Preheat the oven to 170°C /340°F/gas mark 3. Grate the rind from half a lemon and season two pieces of plaice with lemon rind, salt and pepper. Roll up and secure each fillet with a cocktail stick. Place the fillets in a casserole dish, sprinkle with assorted chopped fresh herbs and cover with any remaining grated rind plus two teaspoons of lemon juice. Cover with a lid. Bake for 40-50 minutes. When the fish is completely white and flakes easily, lift it out and transfer it to a warmed serving dish. Serve with a green salad.

• Chicken stir-fry makes a quick supper dish. Heat 1 tablespoon of sunflower oil or olive oil in a non-stick frying pan and partly cook 110g (4oz) sliced chicken breast until it changes colour. Add 1 medium tin beansprouts, 3 sticks finely sliced celery, 1 Spanish onion, peeled and sliced, and 85g (3oz) mushrooms, washed and sliced, a little at a time until all the ingredients are lightly cooked. Serve with 85g (3oz) boiled brown rice.

Delicious desserts

• Baked apples. Preheat the oven to 175°C/350°F/gas mark 4. Cut a ring in the peel around the middle of a large cooking apple and remove the core. Stuff the core with $^{1}/_{2}$ tablespoon finely chopped Brazil nuts, 1 tablespoon sultanas and $^{1}/_{2}$ teaspoon each of ground cinnamon and ground coriander, place in an ovenproof dish and bake for 35 minutes. Delicious served with low-fat yogurt.

• For a fruit fool, put 2 punnets strawberries, 2 cartons low-fat yogurt, 1 teaspoon honey and 1 teaspoon natural vanilla essence into a liquidizer and blend until smooth. Serve in a tall glass, sprinkled with flaked almonds or chopped Brazil nuts.

Daily Treatments

Whether you want a flatter stomach to make you feel better, to hold your posture better or

to give you more self-confidence, the aim of this programme is to show you how

it can be done with the minimum of pain.

However, there are certain things that you should do each day.

Stretch

Greet each day with an early morning stretch either in bed or first thing when you get up. Stress, watching too much TV, even lying in bed for up to eight hours can all cause muscular aches and pains to develop. Inactivity can ultimately lead to a build-up of lactic acid in the muscles resulting in pain and stiffness. That is why the daily routine of stretching the arms and body is invaluable.

Energy shower

There is nothing quite like an early morning energy shower to kick-start the body into

action, so try each morning to jump into the shower and, if you are feeling brave enough, when you are ready to come out, turn the cold tap full on for several minutes.

After showering, stimulate your body and boost the circulation by slapping your skin all over. Using the flats of your hands slap from toes to hip, wrist to shoulder and all over your chest, shoulders and torso before rubbing yourself dry with a towel.

Wake-up drink

Don't forget to start the day with a glass of hot water with an added squeeze of lemon or lime to cleanse your mouth and put a zing in your step.

Exercise

The various types of exercise recommended for toning and strengthening the abdominal area were

Make sure that each day you:
- Have a morning stretch
- Take a daily energy shower
- Start the day with a glass of water with a squeeze of lemon or lime juice
- Focus on an inspiring thought appropriate to each day
- Spend 30 minutes exercising
- Include some stomach exercises
- Do 10-15 mini sit-ups each day
- Spend five minutes practising quality breathing
- Each day pamper yourself in some special way

discussed previously. Don't forget that they form a critical part of the programme and so should be included every day, even if you don't always feel in the mood. Try to build up the number you can manage gradually day by day.

Inspiring thoughts

When was the last time you seriously thought about yourself and your life? Last week? Last month? Perhaps you can't even remember the last time. Why not make a determined effort throughout this programme to allow yourself some quality time to think about your future and what you would like to achieve? It could be something as wacky as doing a bungee jump, or perhaps you would like to start a business of your own, or spend a weekend at a health farm. All of these things are attainable – none need remain a pipe dream. We all need goals in life to aim at, and so why not allow yourself 10 minutes each day to sit down and write how you feel and to record something that you would like to do in the future. It doesn't matter if it sounds weird or bizarre. If that's how you feel, write it down in your diary as an inspiring thought for the day.

Deep breathing

There is nothing quite as invigorating or refreshing as five minutes of deep steady breathing. It blows away those cobwebs and is also an excellent way to de-stress yourself.

1. Sit in a quiet room.
2. If you are wearing a skirt or trousers, undo the waistband so there is plenty of room for you to expand your tummy.
3. Close your eyes, now slowly breathe in through your nose and hold that breath for a count of five. Then, to another count of five, slowly exhale through your mouth.
4. Repeat several times until the 5 minutes are up.

Pamper yourself

And why not? You deserve it; you're a good person, so go out and treat yourself to the biggest, brightest bunch of flowers you can find, book yourself in for a hair appointment, spend one afternoon sifting through your old collections of books and records, or clear out your wardrobe. Whatever takes your fancy, just make sure you allow time for yourself each day.

Good posture

Good posture is achievable. It will not only make you feel better but you will look smarter too.

Here are some simple steps to help you to improve your posture:

1. When walking, make a conscious effort to keep your backbone straight and hold your shoulders back. Pull in your stomach and buttocks and tuck in your chin.
2. When seated, sit up straight and do not cross your legs.
3. If working at a desk choose a seat in which you are comfortable and which is at the correct position for your desk. The seat should be high enough to allow your thighs to rest horizontally on the seat.
4. Wear sensible low-heeled shoes. Keep high ones for the occasional night out. Shoes with low heels put far less strain on your back than stiletto heels.
5. Practise walking around the house with a heavy book balanced on your head, as though you were at a deportment class. The aim is to reach the other end of the room with the book still on your head

Maintaining The Programme

Trying to change is never easy and there are bound to be occasions during the 28 days when you think 'Why bother? What is the point of it all?' When you have one of those days, sit down and spend a little longer on finding an inspiring thought to lift your spirits.

Remind yourself that you are doing the programme because you want to wear a cropped top again on your holidays, you want to feel more confident in how you look, you want get rid of that surplus bulge around your midriff which has been reluctant to move since you had your last child.

The 28 day plan is not meant to be an ordeal. Yes, you will have to be prepared for a little hard work at times, but it should not be something you dread doing. It is important that you set aside an hour or so each day for a bit of personal TLC. On these pages, I suggest various ideas for making you feel good about yourself.

Flower power

Studies carried out in America have shown that if you surround yourself with flowers, they can trigger off feelings of happiness, soothe away anxieties and improve your quality of life. So if Mr Right has not bought you a bunch recently, take the initiative and buy yourself some.

Reading

Choose a really good novel and curl up one afternoon for a couple of hours to read it. If it makes you cry, so much the better – everyone needs a good cry now and then. It can help to relieve stress.

Hand pampering

If your hands are feeling slightly dry and could do with some pampering, mix a teaspoon of honey with two teaspoons of olive oil and massage it into your hands after washing them in warm soapy water and

How to lift negative emotions
• Keep a record of those negative thoughts. Write them down in a diary and then shut to challenge them by putting positive messages alongside.
'I don't feel that I'm looking any better' may be a negative message, 'but you are doing a lot more than before and are much fitter' could be the positive reply.
• If you have times when you feel anxious or stressed out, stop and think about happy occasions and try to remember how they felt
• Ignore negative thoughts whenever they worm their way into your mind. After all, millions of thoughts pass through our minds each day; thoughts can't harm you.
• Set yourself a challenge – take up a new sport and aspire to a certain level of proficiency. By achieving this, you will feel much more confident of your abilities.

rying them gently. Pop a pair of cotton gloves on
nd go to bed wearing the gloves, allowing the oil to
oak in overnight In the morning wash your hands in
varm soapy water. They will feel soft and clean.

urf the internet

Jave you often wished that you could surf the net,
ut you are frustrated because you don't know the
irst thing about it? Well, now's the time to change all

Minty bath
If you are looking for a bath with a difference then
try this one. You need:
• 1 cup chopped fresh mint
• 1 cup chopped bay leaves
• 1 teaspoon coconut oil
• 1 teaspoon almond extract
Add all the ingredients into a bowl and stir well.
Cut a piece of cheesecloth or similar material into
a large square and tie it into a pouch. Drop the
ingredients into the middle of the square and tie
the ends together. When drawing the hot water for
a bath, dip the pouch into the flowing water and
allow the herbs time to infuse. Once the water has
cooled down to a comfortable temperature, step
into the bath and relax for 30 minutes.

that! If you have a computer and modem at home,
there is no time like the present to learn a new skill.
There are lots of books in the library telling you how
to get online, and some local colleges run short
introductory courses on the subject. Once you have a
basic understanding, you will find that the internet
opens up a whole new world to you.

Thinking positive

You may well face days during the programme when
you are plagued by negative thoughts, but hidden
beneath those dull feelings are positive emotions
lying in wait. So work hard each day to bring them to
the fore. When you feel good about yourself, you can
begin to understand and accept the type of person
you are and not punish yourself mentally for any
shortcomings or imperfections. We are all human,
after all. Experts have found that people who are
positive and optimistic enjoy long-term good health.

Flat Stomach: Days 1–7

You've done all the preparatory work and now can look forward to a 28-day programme that should leave you feeling invigorated and rejuvenated.

Whether you are a working woman or a busy mother at home, the next 28 days should witness some of the biggest changes that you will ever make to your life...so be prepared! Draw up a chart (see page 157) and stick it on your fridge or kitchen wall so that you will remember exactly what you must include on each day of your programme.

Keep a diary and record in it your everyday thoughts. Even if you have had a rotten day, write it down and then try to understand why it was such a bad day. At the end of each day summarize how you feel. Naturally on some days you will find more to write about than on others, but it will help to keep you motivated if you keep this diary and refer to it for encouragement when you have down days.

One good tip to keep you motivated is to take a skirt out of your wardrobe, one that is slightly too cosy around the waist, and call it 'the flabby skirt'. Make a record of your measurements on the first day of your programme and pin it on to the waistband of the skirt. Whenever you have moments of self-doubt, remind yourself of how nice it would be to wear that skirt without it pinching. That ambition is achievable.

Here is a typical plan for day 1, but of course times and the order in which activities are performed may differ, according to your individual lifestyle.

7.00am Early morning stretch – spend 10 minutes stretching and flexing those tired, stiff muscles. Open your bedroom window and let in some fresh air before you begin.

7.15am Refresh your mouth and body with a glass of hot water to which a squeeze of fresh lemon juice has been added.

8.00am Have an energy shower.

8.45am Time for breakfast. Why not just eat fruit this morning?

9.30am Go for a brisk 30-minute power walk.

11.00am Have a glass of water and spend five minutes on quality breathing.

1.00pm Lunch. Try a beetroot salad.

2.15pm Time to do some sit-ups. Just aim to do ten today and remember to include the warm-up and cooling-down exercises too. Afterwards relax and read a book with a cup of herbal tea.

4.00pm Find a quiet place, sit down and think about some goal that you would like to achieve within the next few years. Write it down on paper and imagine how it can be attained.

6.00pm Prepare dinner, perhaps some fish this evening. Enjoy a piece of fruit for dessert.

7.00pm Why not indulge in a minty bath and subtly illuminate the bathroom with candles?

8.00pm End the first day by giving your nails a manicure. Then climb into bed with a good book and read for a while until drowsiness overtakes you.

Don't forget: As you complete each activity, tick it off on your chart and before you go to sleep remember to record in your diary how you felt, noting down both the good and the bad points.

Remainder of the week

The remainder of week 1 should follow more or less the same pattern but add some different foods and try different exercises to keep things fresh. Don't try increasing the sit-ups or stomach exercises until the latter part of the week.

Measurements chart

As you change your routine to include more exercise and reform your eating habits, you will find that you are not only achieving a flatter stomach but you will have toned up muscles all over your body to give you a slimmer look and lots more energy!

You can record your measurements each week using this simple chart.

	Week 1	Week 2	Week 3	Week 4
Date				
Weight				
Bust				
Waist				
Hips				

Exercise diary

It is a good idea to keep an exercise diary like the example below. Make a note of the activities you have undertaken and how you felt afterwards and you will soon begin to see clear signs of improvement in stamina and fitness.

Fill it in at the end of each day and by the end of the programme you will see how much more you are able to do than at the beginning.

Week 1	Exercise	Length of time/distance	Comments
1st April	Walking	12 minutes/half a mile	Shattered
2nd April	Walking	10 minutes/half a mile	Breathless
	Sit ups	20 minutes	Exhausted, felt super
3rd April	Swimming	40 minutes/8 lengths	Exhilarated but tired

Flat Stomach: Days 8–14

One week down, only three to go! By now certain routines should be established and you

should be used to the programme.

But remember, no slacking! And don't start eating foods that are banned!

7.00am Early morning stretch – spend 10 minutes stretching and flexing those tired muscles. Open your bedroom window and let in some fresh air before you begin.

7.15am Refresh your mouth and body with a glass of hot water to which a squeeze of lime or lemon juice has been added.

8.00am Take an energy shower or perhaps try having a bath this week doing exactly the same as when showering i.e. turning the cold tap on full and

splashing the cool water over your body before getting out.

8.45am Time for breakfast. Muesli today!

9.30am Spend time doing your stomach exercises. Then have a glass of water; you will almost certainly need it after that workout.

11.00am Perhaps you have had an inspiring idea that you would like to pursue. You could try writing some poetry or a story.

1.00pm Lunch. If you are meeting friends for lunch, then make sure that you choose a low-fat dish, possibly a baked potato or a sandwich containing low-fat ingredients. Remember, read the labels if you

De-stress yourself

When things are getting on top of you and you dread going to bed in case worries and concerns worm their way into your subconscious mind, it is time for action. This is how to relax totally.

• Lie or sit down, whichever feels more comfortable.

• Close your eyes and imagine a favourite room; it could be any room, anywhere. Say to yourself 'Nothing else matters'.

• Concentrate on all the objects in that room that make it so special to you, such as the curtains or the pictures hanging on the walls.

• Now eradicate each and every one of those images one by one until there is nothing at all left. The room is empty.

• Keep this image in your mind for a few moments and while you do so luxuriate in the sensation of total peace and tranquillity. You have never felt so totally relaxed and your mind is free of unwanted thoughts.

are buying pre-packed products. Complement the food with a glass of fresh juice.

2.15pm If you feel guilty at having taken longer than normal over lunch, why not do some power walking for 30 minutes?

4.00pm Get your exercise gear on again for some mini sit-ups. By now you may be in a position to increase the number slightly, but don't rush. Afterwards make sure you cool down and have a glass or two of water to replenish any lost fluids.

6.00pm Prepare dinner. Tonight I suggest a chicken meal with rice.

7.00pm Practise some deep breathing and then pamper yourself – do a crossword, listen to some music, enjoy anything that you find relaxing for an hour or two.

8.00pm It has been a busy day, so have an early

night! If you have trouble getting off to sleep or are plagued by negative thoughts, try the de-stressing routine described below.

Don't forget: As you complete each activity, tick it off on your chart and before you go to sleep remember to record in your diary how you felt, noting down both the good and the bad points.

Remainder of the week

The rest of week 2 should follow more or less the same basic routine, but don't let boredom set in. Set yourself little targets. You might see if there are any local aerobic classes held nearby which you could join. Group activities give you a chance to meet other people and help to keep you motivated. Better still, if your place of work has a gym, why not spend part of your lunchtime working out?

Flat Stomach: Days 15–21

You will by now have established a routine and perhaps made some changes to personalize the programme to suit your lifestyle.

So are you ready for week 3? You are now half-way through the programme and are probably getting used to the new lifestyle.

7.00am Early morning stretch – spend 10 minutes stretching and flexing those tired muscles. Open your bedroom window and let in some fresh air before you begin.

7.15am Refresh your mouth and body with a glass of hot water to which a squeeze of lemon juice has been added.

8.00am Have an energy shower.

8.45am Time for breakfast. Have a muffin with some Marmite on it.

9.30am Why not try another exercise activity this week; you might take up cycling or try some water aerobics. Or you could do some gardening – all the bending is an excellent way of exercising your stomach. Don't forget the warm-up routine beforehand.

11.00am Time to stop for a cup of water and a few minutes' rest. If it's a nice day, you could do some quality breathing whilst sitting in a chair in the sunshine.

1.00pm Lunch. If you have expended energy gardening, you will be feeling pretty hungry so you might prepare yourself a tuna salad with a small low-fat yogurt to follow.

2.15pm Spend about 15 minutes doing mini sit-ups. By now you should easily be able to manage at least 40 sit-ups without adverse effects.

4.00pm By the third week you should have begun to notice that your stomach muscles are looking slightly more toned and you should generally be feeling healthier. You deserve a treat, so go and buy yourself a bunch of flowers.

6.00pm Dinner. A vegetable and chicken stir-fry followed by baked apples is delicious. Try to get someone else to do the dishes and sit down for a while to watch the TV or catch up on that book you've almost finished.

Warm-up gardening exercises

It's amazing how strenuous gardening can be and how much strain it puts on certain parts of the body, especially the back and legs. Make sure before you get down to weeding or mowing the lawn that you do some warm-up exercises beforehand.

1. You will need a good overall stretch. With your hands above your head, stretch as far as you are able sideways, hold for a count of 15 and then stretch to the opposite side, again holding the pose for a count of 15. Relax.

2. The legs, especially the hamstrings, can take some punishment, so you need to stretch them thoroughly. Stand upright and place your hands on one leg just above the knee. Gently lean forward and, making sure the other leg remains straight, bend down slowly. You should feel the stretch in the back of your thigh. Hold for a count of 8, then do the same with the other leg.

3. When you've finished gardening, lie on the floor face-down, slowly lift your upper body a little and stretch backwards. This is the perfect exercise to counteract the strain that your spine has been subjected to after all the forward bending that gardening requires.

7.00pm If, towards the middle of the third week, you are beginning to feel anxious and worried that you won't reach your target, that you're having a rotten day and nothing is going right, your stomach still looks flabby and you've eaten a forbidden chocolate bar, take time out to de-stress.

8.00pm Have an early night – tomorrow will be better!

Don't forget: As you complete each activity, tick it off on your chart and before you go to sleep remember to record in your diary how you felt, noting down both the good and the bad points.

Remainder of the week

Keep up with the routine even if you don't feel like doing it some days. If you hit a bad patch and feel really down in the dumps, do something positive – go out and buy yourself a treat, ask a friend around, or, if you are a mother, take the kids swimming after school. Jump into the water too – the kids will love it and there's no better way of teaching youngsters how much fun exercising can be.

Flat Stomach: Days 22–28

This is it! You are nearing the end of your 28-day Flat Stomach programme and you have survived.
You should begin to feel more energetic now, largely on account of a healthier diet combined
with regular exercise and relaxation.

So don't give up now. Why throw away all your hard-won gains?

7.00am Early morning stretch – spend 10 minutes stretching and flexing those tired muscles. Open your bedroom window and let in some fresh air before you begin.

7.15am Refresh your mouth and body with a glass of hot water to which a squeeze of lime juice has been added.

8.00am Have an energy shower.

8.45am Time for breakfast. Why not choose something hot for a change?

9.30am Time for some stomach workouts. They should be no problem by now.

11.00am Have a cup of herbal tea before popping out to the shops.

1.00pm Lunch. If a friend is coming around, you might prepare some healthy sandwiches.

2.15pm Go out for a cycle ride. Make sure you plan a route that takes you along roads that are not too busy. If you feel embarrassed to be seen cycling around the neighbourhood, you can always pack the bike into your car and drive somewhere quiet for a 30-minute cycle. Remember don't go too far from the car; you need to conserve enough energy to get back

to it at the end of the ride.

4.00pm If you feel exhausted after the cycle ride, do some quality breathing and then recharge your batteries with a glass of freshly squeezed orange juice.

6.00pm Prepare a special meal for family or friends, perhaps pasta with salad. And because it is nearly the end of your programme, you can treat yourself to a glass of wine.

7.00pm Sit down and round off your 'inspiring thought' plan. Leave it for a few days and then go back and review it in the light of the progress you have made over the four-week period.

8.00pm Enjoy a relaxing bath with some favourite essential oils and then have an early night to recover from the exertions of the day.

Don't forget: As you complete each activity, tick it off on your chart and before you go to sleep remember to record in your diary how you felt, noting down both the good and the bad points.

Remainder of the week

Keep up with the routine right through to the very last day. On the final day why not celebrate, and treat yourself to some new exercise gear? If you are feeling really good, from now on exercise will become part of your daily life.

Activity Record Chart

Record your activities every day using this table

DAILY ACTIVITIES	1	2	3	4	5	6	7	8	9	10	11	12	13	14	15	16	17	18	19	20	21	22	23	24	25	26	27	28
Morning stretch																												
Glass of hot water and lemon or lime juice																												
Shower/bath																												
Breakfast																												
Lunch																												
Dinner																												
Fresh vegetables																												
Fresh fruit																												
Protein food																												
450ml (3/4 pint) skimmed or semi-skimmed milk																												
1.75 litres (3 pints) water																												
10 mins inspiring thought																												
10 mins stomach exercises																												
30 mins exercise																												
10–15 mins sit-ups																												
Pampering																												
5 mins quality breathing																												

Congratulations!

Provided you have followed the programme properly and done the exercises as recommended, and not fallen off the wagon and allowed yourself too many 'treats', your hard work should now have paid off and you will be the proud owner of a well-toned flat stomach.

Don't worry if you still have a little way to go to achieve that dream washboard abdomen – remember that everyone's metabolism is different and you have done really well to get this far.

You might now want to jump onto the scales to find out exactly how much weight you have lost. Then try on that flabby skirt that you put to one side and check whether there is now plenty of room for manoeuvre. If you feel happy with the way you look, then you can allow yourself to loosen up a little and relax your eating regime. But be careful! It's very easy to return to old habits.

In order to maintain your new look:
- Continue eating three meals a day
- Try sticking to low-fat foods
- Continue taking regular aerobic exercise
- Remember that good posture is important to how you look
- Make sure that you keep that flabby skirt handy, just in case those extra pounds start to creep back round your waistline again
- Don't become obsessive about your weight; after all, your aim was to tone and strengthen your stomach muscles and, having achieved that, you can be proud of yourself
- Enjoy your new shape

The 28 Day Plan

BUMS AND TUMS

The 28 Day Plan

How many times have you taken a sly backward glance at your rear end in a shop window and
cringed at the shape of it, hardly believing it was attached to your anatomy? The war between
women and their derrières has long been an on-going feud and with the passing of years it
doesn't seem to get much easier.

But don't worry – help is at hand. This 28 day
programme will show you how it is possible to
firm up that bum and tone that tum.

What causes that extra weight?

Hormones, lack of exercise, sluggish circulation,
preparation for child-bearing years – all these play a
part in the reason why women are predisposed to
carrying the body's fat stores in the hip and thigh area.

Extra flesh gained around the abdominal area and
buttocks is difficult to move because once those fat
cells have been formed, although they may shrink,
they are constantly lying in wait, ready to pounce. The
only way to deal with excess flab is to embark on a
combined programme of exercise and healthy eating.

Follow the 28 day plan

Thousands of women complain about their stomach
or buttocks either being too large or out of shape. But
why bemoan the fact that you no longer have the
slender buttocks or flat stomach of an eighteen year
old? Be honest – you'll never see eighteen again, so
isn't it time you stopped wishing and started doing
something positive.

You may never be a teenager again but that
doesn't mean to say you can't restore your figure to a
well toned, lean shape. At the end of this programme
you will feel a totally different person, more
confident, happier, in control of your life and, if not
lighter, you will certainly look it.

Exercise

If you are a confirmed couch potato, now is the time to make some changes in your life, and it isn't as difficult as you might imagine it to be. Experts agree that in order to maintain a healthy body and mind, a minimum of 30 minutes of physical exercise each day is fundamental.

It doesn't necessarily have to be as intensive as swimming or jogging. A brisk walk, gardening or housework are all just as effective and it doesn't have to be done in a 30-minute session. Exercise can be split up into three 10-minute sessions.

As well as toning and strengthening muscles, exercise can:

✓ Improve your overall physical and mental well-being
✓ Help prevent heart disease, high blood pressure, strokes and diabetes (Type 2)
✓ Reduce high blood cholesterol
✓ Guard against osteoporosis
✓ Prevent arthritis setting in
✓ Help improve bad circulation
✓ Relieve stress and anxiety related problems
✓ Improve sleep problems

Whatever your age, before exercising it is important to remember these basic guidelines:

• Exercise at a rate that feels right for you
• Don't exercise when you feel unwell
• Always warm up and cool down to prevent injury
• Don't push yourself too hard – build up gradually
• Check with your GP if you have any medical condition, especially if you are pregnant

Warming Up

Warming up and stretching is a very important part of your workout routine and is essential to avoid injuries. Your warm up routine should increase your heart-rate and relax your muscles.

Warm up exercises prevent the possibility of damaging muscles. Equally important is to finish off with the same routine, enabling the body to cool down and return to its normal heartbeat. Ideally the routine should only take between 5-10 minutes to perform.

Shoulders

To loosen up tense shoulder and neck muscles, stand with feet slightly apart with your weight on the left foot, Roll the left shoulder backwards 10 times then the right shoulder, changing weight from the left foot to the right foot.

Arms and knees

This is a great one for posture. Stand up straight, tummy tucked in, then swing both arms up and then down, bending the knees as you bring the arms down in a gentle smooth action. Repeat 14 times.

Side to side

Stand with feet evenly spaced apart, knees gently bent and with hands firmly on hips. Very slowly lean over to one side, stretching the arm out at the same time as far as you can. Return to standing position and do the other side. Repeat 4 stretches on each side.

Waisting time

This is a great one for the spine and waist. Stand with feet slightly apart, knees gently bent and hips facing forward. Raise the arms almost to shoulder level and,

taking it easy, twist the body from side to side. Do 4 twists on each side.

Arm stretch

Sit on the floor cross-legged. Place one hand slightly behind you, and bring the other arm up, palm outward facing, stretching as far as you are able. Hold to the count of 8, bring the arm back down and repeat with the other arm.

Body stretch

This is a rather pleasant exercise. Simply lie on your back and stretch your arms and legs as far as possible. Hold for 5 seconds and then relax.

Where to exercise?

Exercising should be fun, enjoyable and something that makes you feel energized and invigorated afterwards. But sometimes it can be lonely and, especially for the social butterfly, rather isolating, in which case it is a good idea to spend some time at the local gym working out on their equipment.

The advantages of exercising in a gym are:

• You meet up with other like-minded people

• You can try out different pieces of equipment

• There are always qualified fitness experts on hand to help you

The disadvantages of exercising in a gym might be:

• You may at first feel embarrassed being amongst other people

• Joining a gym or even enrolling for several classes can prove expensive

• You may feel under pressure to push yourself

Working out at home also has advantages and disadvantages.

At home there is often the luxury of:

• Working totally at your own pace

• Wearing any old clothes and not feeling intimated by the trendy sportswear of others

• It's cheaper

The disadvantages of exercising at home might be:

• It is lonely and can often be boring

• You may need outside stimulation and motivation

• There is no-one to check that you are doing the exercises correctly

• You won't have the availability of the varied equipment in the gym

Choosing to work alone or go along to a gym is purely an individual decision. However, if at any time throughout the programme you feel your enthusiasm is waning slightly, it may be a good idea to pop along to a gym for moral support.

Home help exercising

Being a housewife is a full-time job and often there are not enough hours in the day to fit in all the tasks you have to do. Surprisingly enough, all those boring mundane household chores such as vacuuming, sweeping and dusting can add up to a quite a strenuous exercise routine, the type that health experts view as potentially being more beneficial than a proper workout. Naturally the harder you work at dusting or vacuuming, the more calories you burn and the better the results are.

Stairs: forget about investing in a step machine when you have your very own. Carrying clothes upstairs, bringing laundry down, going upstairs to make the beds, bringing litter bins down – all are ideal for strengthening leg muscles.

Vacuuming: spend a morning vacuuming – perfect toning exercise for the arms and back.

Walkies: take the dog for a 30-minute walk each day – perfect all-round exercise. If you don't have a dog, borrow a neighbour's.

Dusting: some people work out better with music so play your favourite music whilst you dust and it will help you to put more effort into the cleaning.

The Exercises

Before you start to exercise the abdominal and buttock muscles, it is important

to understand how they work.

The stomach muscles

Basically the stomach area is made up of four main abdominal muscles:

Obliques, internal and external: Two diagonal lengths of muscle called the external and internal obliques run across the front of the ribs and around to the spine. Their primary function is to help the torso when twisting, bending from side to side and to help keep it stable.

Transversus abdominus (deep): Running horizontally from the lower ribs to the spine, this group of muscles holds and maintains the shape of the internal organs. Each time we are told to hold the tummy in, it is these muscles which activate the action.

Rectus abdominus (front): A muscle that runs vertically from the sternum to the pubic bone, its main role is to help ease moving the torso from a lying down position to an upright one.

Problems occur as weight creeps on around the midsection and the muscles become engulfed beneath, losing the ability to retain their former defined shape. As more weight settles then it doesn't matter if you wear a girdle, or hold your stomach in all day – it won't make any difference as the fat is there to stay unless you do something about it, and that means exercise.

Types of exercise for the stomach area

There are two main types of exercise that will help in attaining a flat stomach both equally as important.

Aerobics: helps to burn fat and involves any form of exercise that makes you feel a little out of breath.

Includes boxercise, cycling, jazz dancing, jogging, power walking, running, skipping and swimming.

Toning or strengthening exercises: work on building up specific muscle areas and in doing so increase the rate at which calories are used up.

Handy hints for a flabby stomach

Learning how to pull your abdominal muscles in can help strengthen them.

• With the stomach muscles relaxed, measure and cut a length of ribbon or string to fit the waist and tie it around.

• As you breathe out pull the navel in, the objective is to keep any tension off the string by maintaining this hold. Take five breaths then exhale. Repeat eight times.

Practise makes perfect and this isn't easy, but when you have achieved holding your stomach in flat without relying on the string it will come as second nature, even when exercising, and ultimately this will ensure you get the best from every workout.

Toning and strengthening exercises

There are many different toning and strengthening exercises which are perfect for the abs. You should try doing each of these exercises slowly and carefully, concentrating on the areas which you are working

and doing 5-10 minutes each day, building up to about 20 minutes. And don't forget before you begin to do a warm-up routine.

Crunch

The basic exercise for strengthening and toning the upper abdominals.

1. Lie with your back flat on the floor, knees bent, tummy tucked in tightly and feet spaced shoulder width apart.

2. Place your hands behind your ears.

3. Now for the difficult part, keep your eyes focused directly on the ceiling and with your elbows wide apart, slowly raise your shoulders off the ground slightly, pulling in the stomach muscles as you do so. Then slowly lower back to the floor. Remember to breathe out as you raise and breathe in as you lower.

4. Repeat as many times as you are able, until you feel a little discomfort. It is not the quantity of crunches that matters, but the quality.

Tip: If you find tummy crunches rather difficult, spend 3 minutes lying flat on your back, pressing your spine into the floor and holding tight to the count of ten.

Doing twenty a day should enable you to progress on to trying a few tummy crunches.

Do not try to do too much too soon.

Pelvic tilt

1. Lie flat on the floor, making sure your neck and shoulders are resting on the floor.
2. Using your stomach muscles, press your lower back down into the floor and at the same time tilt your pubic bone upwards.
3. Pull your stomach in towards the floor and hold for the count of five.
4. Repeat 12 times.

Basic sit-ups

Basic sit-ups are ideal for anyone who hasn't done any abdominal exercises for a while.
1. Lie on the floor, legs bent and feet placed hip width apart, with soles flat on the floor.
2. Cup your hands gently on the back of your neck. Inhale, then as you exhale, use your abdominal muscles to lift your body a few centimetres off the floor. Hold the position for a few seconds, then lower back down slowly to the starting position.

Full sit-ups

1. Lie on the floor in the same position as for the crunch, with hands gently resting behind your ears. Do not be tempted to hold on to your head or neck in any way.
2. Now raise your whole body up slowly, remembering to exhale as you rise up and keeping the feet flat on the ground. The aim of this exercise is to sit upright, but very few people manage this in the beginning so don't worry, just go as far as you feel able to without feeling any undue strain placed on your back.
3. Slowly roll back down to the floor, remembering to exhale.
4. Then relax, and have another try.

Remember that it is more beneficial to raise up a little way and hold the position for a few seconds than to sit more upright and lower to quickly.

Tip: If you don't feel your abdominal muscles engage as you lift, then you are not doing the exercise correctly. Work at your own pace and aim to do only as many as you feel comfortable.

Exercising the buttocks

Saggy, large, voluptuous or a well-toned derrière? Which would you prefer to have? For most women the sight of an emerging derrière does little to make them feel self-confident, especially if those muscles are flabby.

The good news is: firming up your rear isn't as difficult as you would imagine. The most effective way to burn off excess fat around the buttocks is to work the body aerobically and to learn exercises that will increase muscle and at the same time reduce fat. Most exercise experts recommend squats that not only work on the front but also get to work firming and toning the bum area too.

There are many reasons for a flabby bum:
- Age
- Childbirth
- A sedentary lifestyle

The buttocks

It is important is to know a little about those buttock muscles.

Gluteus maximus: This forms the main bulk of the buttocks and is generally used when making strong movements such as climbing the stairs and running.

Gluteus medius: A thick muscle found over the posterior and which is covered by the gluteus maximus. Its main role is to rotate the thigh.

Types of exercise

Similar to those abdominal muscles which have been left to turn flabby, the best way to deal with flabby buttock muscles is a combined programme of healthy eating and exercise. It isn't really as difficult as you imagine, provided you choose those exercises designed for the lower part of the body.

Here is a selection to try, but before each session remember to do some warm-up exercises.

Lunges

1. Stand with feet hip width apart, palms facing in towards the body.
2. Take one long step forward and bend both knees so the front knee is aligned with the ankle and the back heel is slightly lifted.
3. Don't allow your back knee to touch the floor as you push yourself up.
4. Then do the same with the other leg.
5. Repeat 10 times on each leg.

Kick back

1. Take up a position on all fours on. Make sure your weight is evenly distributed.
2. Lift your right leg up behind you until the thigh is parallel to the floor and the lower leg is raised straight up into the air at 90 degrees to the thigh. Do not lift your thigh higher than parallel to the floor as this would be stressful to the lower back.
3. Breathe in as you raise the leg and breathe out as you return to the starting position.
4. Repeat the movement 9 times before beginning 10 repetitions with the left leg.

Remember to hold your stomach muscles in tight to help support your back. Keep your head and spine straight and look straight ahead. Your aim is to work up to 25 kick backs with each leg by the end of the 28 day programme, but only increase the repetitions when you feel ready.

Squats

Squats are ideal for helping to tone up the buttocks.
1. Stand with both legs shoulder width apart, feet parallel.
2. Crossing the arms in front of your chest, inhale as you go down into a squat but go no lower than the point at which your thighs are parallel to the floor. Make sure the head and back are kept straight.
3. As you stand up, exhale and straighten legs completely.
4. Repeat 12-15 times.

Intermediate squats

1. Stand with your stomach in, back straight and chest lifted.

2. Tilt your pelvis forward and, as you inhale, bend your knees and hips and gradually go into a squat position.

3. Maintain your weight over your ankles, keep your head up with your chin parallel to the floor and look directly to the front.

4. As you remain steady in the squat position, reach your arms straight out in front at shoulder level. Make sure your back is still kept straight, chest lifted, knees aligned with your feet and thighs parallel to the ground.

5. As you gradually stand up, exhale and keep your back straight and feet flat on the floor.

6. Repeat 12–15 times

Worktime workouts

If you are seated at a desk for 7 hours a day, then neither the buttocks nor the abs are getting very much exercise. However, there are some activities which you can do whilst at work.

The squeeze: Stand up and as you do so squeeze the muscles in your buttocks until you feel unable to do it any further, then gradually sit back down in your seat. Try to do this every time you stand up, when at the filing cabinet, standing to take a phone call, standing at the kitchen sink, etc. This is the perfect exercise for toning up both the legs and buttocks.

Leg work: This exercise will work the front of the thighs and the muscles in the back of the thighs. While sitting at your desk rest your left heel against your right toes. Gradually straighten out your right leg and at the same time, push back on it with the left leg. Once the leg is straight, reverse the movement with the left leg.

Outdoor exercise

As with the abs, the buttocks also respond to aerobic forms of exercise and often a mixture of indoor workouts and exercising outdoors lessens the possibility of boredom setting in. If the idea of jogging or cycling holds little appeal, there are plenty of other exercises to get the adrenaline going.

Exercises to help tone up the abs and buttocks:

✓ Brisk walking	✓ Skipping	✓ Kick boxing
✓ Dancing	✓ Squash	✓ Tennis
✓ Gardening	✓ Swimming	✓ Housework

A Healthy Diet

The 28 day plan is not a diet, there is no calorie counting, weighing food or checking portions, but to ensure positive results, it is important simply to follow a healthy eating programme.

By cutting back on some foods that are known to contain excess fat it is easy to follow a balanced low-fat diet which contains all the nutrients your body needs to maintain health and provide you with the energy you need.

Nourishing the body

Changing eating habits can be great fun and because no single food provides all the necessary nutrients to enable the body to work at its optimum level it needs a variety to provide the correct balance of essential carbohydrates, proteins, vitamins, minerals and fat.

Carbohydrates: these provide energy for the body and come in two basic varieties: simple carbohydrates (which include basically sugar and very little else) and complex carbohydrates (which include starchy foods such as bread, potatoes, cereal, pasta and rice).

Fat: number one enemy for the body but also essential for helping to insulate and protect the organs and nerves. It is found in varying quantities in numerous foods such as butter, cheese, lard, dripping, snack foods, fatty meat, etc. The basic aim of a healthy eating diet is to reduce the amount of fat you eat and stick to a low-fat diet but this doesn't mean cutting out all fat, simply choosing those foods sensibly and checking on the label for low fat.

Proteins: the body breaks down the protein from food into its component building blocks called amino acids which build and repair tissue and muscle. Found in foods such as meat, poultry, fish, dairy foods, cheese, yogurt, eggs, beans, lentils, nuts, and cereals.

Vitamins: vital for good health and various bodily functions. A well-balanced diet containing plenty of fresh fruits and vegetables should be rich in vitamins.

Minerals: essential for forming bones, strengthening teeth, maintaining a healthy immune system and supporting the vitamins in their work. Calcium is important for helping to build strong bones and teeth.

Low-fat food

Whilst on this 28 day programme there are certain favourite foods you will have to forfeit but with such a wide and varied amount of choice available that won't seem too much of a hardship unless you are a slave to cakes and chocolate and all those 'naughty but nice foods'. While you are abstaining remember the reason for doing so – a well-toned abdomen and firm buttocks.

There are several ways to make things a little easier when cutting back on the fat content in your food: When shopping make sure you always pay attention to the nutritional content listed on the packaging. The two most important details are the total fat and energy content.

The energy values will be shown in kilojoules or kilocalories (kcal). The kcal figure tells you the number of calories per 100g (4oz). Try to select food containing no more than 4g (0.14oz) of fat per 100g of weight. Don't be tempted by those foods that simply say they are low fat – always check the label to confirm this for yourself.

• Use semi-skimmed or skimmed milk.
• Steam, grill or bake foods instead of frying whenever possible.
• Use low-fat yogurt in place of cream, ice cream or evaporated milk.

Each day on the programme make sure you eat:
✓ Three meals a day: breakfast, lunch, dinner
✓ 175g (6oz) protein food (fish, poultry, meat, cottage cheese)
✓ 350g (12oz) vegetables
✓ 350g (12oz) fresh fruit (including fruit juice)
✓ 175g (6oz) bread, cereal, potatoes, rice, pasta
✓ 450ml (³/4 pint) skimmed or semi-skimmed milk

• Eat cottage cheese instead of full-fat cheese.
• Add more fish and poultry to your diet.
• Always trim visible fat from meat.
• Simmer food in vegetable stock instead of shallow-frying in lard or butter.

Obviously you need a small amount of fat in your diet but at least by following these brief guidelines you are making sure you won't get too much.

Banned foods

If you are really serious about following this plan then there are certain types of foods that are banned, unless in very special circumstances they are unavoidable:

Meats

- Black pudding
- Fat or skin from all meat and poultry
- Goose and other fatty meat
- Haggis

- Pâté
- Pork pie
- Salami
- Sausage
- Scotch eggs

Dairy produce

- All cheese, except cottage cheese
- Butter
- Cream
- Dripping
- Egg custard
- Eggs and other related products
- Full-fat milk

- Ice cream
- Lard
- Low-fat spreads containing more than 4 per cent fat and all similar products
- Margarine
- Quiches
- Suet

Other foods

- All fried foods
- Avocados
- Biscuits
- Cakes
- Chocolate
- Chocolate spread
- Cocoa and related products
- Crisps
- Fudge
- Lemon curd

- Marzipan
- Pastries – sweet and savoury
- Peanut butter
- Sauces and dressings which contain cream, whole milk or eggs
- Sponge puddings
- Sweets
- Toffees

What you can have

It's not all bad news as there are many tempting and tasty foods that you can enjoy throughout the programme and lots of delicious menus to experiment with. For example:

Bread: choose wholemeal.

Cottage cheese: you don't have to stick with the plain variety – choose ones flavoured with chives or pineapple provided they are of the low-fat variety and not made with fresh cream. They make a refreshing addition to a salad or can be spread on crispbreads for a quick lunchtime snack. Add a handful of herbs and garlic to plain cottage cheese for a tasty dip.

Gravy: if you can't possibly survive a meal without gravy, make sure it is made using gravy powder and not from the meat juices.

Pasta and rice: nutritious and satisfying but whenever possible stick to the wholemeal varieties

Vegetables: you can choose whatever you like, even potatoes – just don't fry them or add butter! And eaten raw, carrots, celery and peapods are all very tasty.

Extras: And to add extra flavour to bread or salads, to pour over fish or pep up a pasta dish, choose from:

- Brown, chilli, horseradish, mint or Worcester sauces
- Fat-free salad dressings
- Lemon juice
- Marmite

- Mustard
- Oil-free vinaigrette
- Soy sauce
- Vinegar

Water is essential for:
- ✓ The digestion of food
- ✓ The elimination of waste products
- ✓ Acting as a lubricant for joints and eyes
- ✓ The regulation of the body's temperature
- ✓ Flushing out kidney and bladder infections
- ✓ Improving the complexion

Drinks

Maintaining a healthy balance of fluid is as important, if not more so, than food and although there seems conflicting advice on the amount of water one should drink in a day, the experts recommend a minimum of 1.5-2 litres (3-4 pints).

If plain water doesn't appeal to you, add a squeeze of lemon or lime juice to give it an extra zing. And provided you follow a healthy well-balanced diet, you will find that most of the food we eat contains a certain amount of fluid. In fact, roughly one-third of an adult's daily fluid intake is actually supplied by the food eaten, broken down as follows:

- Tea and coffee provide just over 62%
- Yogurt and milk provide just over 10%
- Bread, cereals, etc provide just over 8%
- Meat, fish and eggs provide 2%
- Fruit and vegetables provide 18%

Other Drinks

There are lots of other refreshing drinks that you can buy or, better still, make in your own kitchen using fruits and vegetables with the added knowledge that fresh fruit and vegetable juices contain the same nutrients and enzymes as in their true form but are easier to digest.

Your New Eating Plan

Not many people like change but the one thing about this programme is that all the

changes made are healthy and nutritious and will make you think more about

the food you and your family are eating.

Number of calories

Calories are needed for energy which the body needs to move, work, keep warm and to function correctly. The food we eat and the liquid we drink is capable of providing all the elements required to keep healthy, but the number of calories the body requires in a day is different for every person. A very broad basic average is that most people consume, on average 2,000 calories every day, although depending on your

weight, height, gender, age, metabolic rate and lifestyle, your body may need more or less.

There are three main factors to consider when calculating the number of calories your body requires each day:

Basal metabolic rate: the amount of energy your body needs to function when at rest. This accounts for 60-70% of calories burned in a day and includes the energy required to keep the heart beating, the lungs breathing, the eyelids blinking and the body temperature stabilized.

Physical activity: this consumes the next highest amount of calories. Physical activity includes everything from making your bed in the morning to walking, jogging, even lifting and moving around the house burns up calories but the exact number depends on the individual person.

Thermic effect on food: this is the amount of energy your body uses to digest the food you eat and break it down to its basic elements to be used by the body.

The next consideration is where you get those calories from.

Breakfast

Clever women eat breakfast and not just a slice of toast or a rushed cup of coffee on the way out to work or taking the children to school. It doesn't have to be a grand affair, just nutritious and healthy. Here are a few ideas for healthy options:

• 2 Weetabix with 1 teaspoon sugar and 100ml (3^1/$_2$fl oz) skimmed milk plus a glass of unsweetened orange juice.
• 175g (6oz) fresh fruit salad with 25g (1oz) unsweetened muesli and 1 small pot low-fat yogurt, plus a glass of unsweetened apple or orange juice.
• Slice of wholemeal toast with 1 teaspoon low-fat spread, served with one medium glass of orange juice.
• 50g (2oz) cornflakes with 1 teaspoon sugar and 100g (4oz) fresh fruit, plus a glass of unsweetened fruit juice.

Muesli

Try making your own muesli the night before.
85ml (3fl oz) skimmed or semi-skimmed milk
6 sultanas
15g (^{1}/$_2$oz) porridge oats
150ml (5fl oz) natural yogurt
1 teaspoon clear honey
Mix all the ingredients together in a bowl. Cover and place in the refrigerator until the morning.

Fruity Choices

• 150ml (5fl oz) low-fat natural yogurt with 1 small banana and a glass of unsweetened fruit juice.
• 300g (11oz) grapefruit in natural juice plus a glass of unsweetened fruit juice or a cup of herbal tea.
• 150ml (5fl oz) low-fat yogurt and a small wedge of melon with a glass of unsweetened fruit juice.

Something Hot

• 115g (4oz) baked beans, 2 grilled tomatoes, 2 grilled turkey rashers together with a 150ml (5fl oz) low-fat yogurt.
• 200g (7oz) can of baked beans on 1 slice of wholemeal toast plus 150ml (5fl oz) low-fat yogurt.
• 1 wholemeal muffin and a piece of fresh fruit with a cup of herbal tea.

Lunch

Eating at lunchtime can be a chore and many people take the easy way out and go to the local corner shop for a pre-packaged sandwich, a packet of crisps and a fizzy drink – not a healthy choice, especially when making up something at home is much cheaper and more nutritious.

Sandwiches can be a great choices provided they contain healthy fillings, so here are some suggestions using two slices of unbuttered wholemeal bread:

• 50g (2oz) skinless chicken, 1 tomato, lettuce and 5ml (1 teaspoon) low-fat yogurt
• 50g (2oz) lean ham and 1 tablespoon apple sauce
• 50g (2oz) tuna in brine, drained, and 1 tomato
• 1 hard-boiled egg, chopped and mixed with 1 tablespoon low-fat natural yogurt and 1 tablespoon reduced oil salad dressing
• 25g (1oz) low fat cottage cheese and 1 sliced banana
• Lay 25g (1oz) wafer-thin ham, half a thinly sliced fresh onion and one sliced tomato on one slice of bread, then place the other slice on top and pop it into a microwave on full power for approximately 1 minute.

Speedy options
In a hurry and looking for something different?

Greek lunch
Crush 1 clove of garlic and mix with 50ml (2fl oz) low-fat Greek yogurt and 2 tablespoons of grated cucumber. Season with salt and pepper and serve with two wholemeal pitta breads, cut into strips.

Baked potatoes
The ideal instant nutritious meal with a range of options to use as fillings:
• Put 100g (4oz) low-fat cottage cheese, 2 tablespoons low-fat yogurt, 1 teaspoon garlic purée and 1 teaspoon dried herbs in a bowl and mix well. Spoon into the cooked potato.
• 50g (2oz) low-fat cottage cheese mixed with 25g (1oz) tuna in brine, drained, and 1 tablespoon low-fat salad dressing.
• 50g (2oz) prawns blended with 50g (2oz) sweetcorn, 1 tablespoon tomato ketchup and 1 tablespoon reduced oil salad dressing.
• 115g (4oz) baked beans with 1/4 teaspoon chilli powder mixed in.
• 200g (7oz) baked beans and salsa (mix together 1 chopped tomato, 1 tablespoon chopped red onion, 2 tablespoons sweetcorn and 1 tablespoon chopped parsley). When the ingredients are well blended spoon the beans into the baked potato and add the salsa.

> **If you really find it difficult to curb those cravings for sugary foods, try snacking on fruit, such as:**
> • 100g (4oz) cherries • 140g (4 1/2oz) plums
> • 90g (3 1/2oz) grapes • 200g (7oz) blackberries
> • 120g (4 1/2oz) pear • 100g (4 oz) melon
> • Large grapefruit • 200g (7oz) strawberries
> • Small banana • Apple

Dinner
By evening, you will be ready for a more substantial meal with the family.

Spaghetti bolognese
Always a family favourite – here's a quick, low-fat recipe, enough for four.
450g (1 lb) lean minced beef
1 large onion, peeled and chopped
1/2 teaspoon dried garlic
1 teaspoon chilli powder
1/2 teaspoon Tabasco sauce
1 tablespoon brown sauce
2 tablespoons tomato ketchup
1 tablespoon tomato purée
400g (14oz) can chopped tomatoes

In a non-stick frying pan dry-fry the mince for approximately 12 minutes and keep stirring until the meat changes colour. Drain the meat through a sieve to make sure all the fat has gone. Using a piece of kitchen paper, wipe out the frying pan before adding the onion and dry-frying until soft and brown. Return the mince to the frying pan and all the remaining ingredients. Mix thoroughly and cook on a low heat for 45 minutes, giving it the occasional stir. Serve with spaghetti and salad.

Tarragon and tuna pasta

Serves one

50g (2oz) wholewheat pasta
185g (6^1/$_2$oz) canned tuna in brine, drained
1 tablespoon fresh tarragon
1 tablespoon cider vinegar
1 tablespoon tomato ketchup
50g (2oz) canned peas
50g (2oz) canned sweetcorn
1 tomato, chopped
Freshly ground black pepper

Cook the pasta in boiling salted water for 8 minutes.
Flake the tuna and mix in the tarragon, cider vinegar
and ketchup. Mix the peas, sweetcorn, tomato, tuna
and the tarragon mixture together in a saucepan and
heat thoroughly. Season with freshly ground
black pepper.

Pasta delight

Serves four

400g (14oz) can tomatoes
Bunch of fresh basil
1 clove garlic
1 carrot, peeled and chopped
1 onion, peeled and chopped
1 pepper (green, red or yellow)
225g (8oz) pasta shapes
6 mushrooms, chopped
Salt and pepper

Put tomatoes, basil, garlic, carrot, onion and pepper
into a food processor and whizz until it forms into a
sauce. Pop the pasta into a saucepan filled with
boiling water and cook for approximately 8 minutes,
then drain. Put the sauce in a saucepan, add the
sliced mushrooms, season and heat. Stir in the pasta,
heat thoroughly and serve.

Daily Treatments

There's an old saying – no pain no gain – that is often true but this programme isn't meant to be a diet or a restricted way of living, you shouldn't feel miserable but enjoy each day and look forward to trying new experiences.

This 28-day plan is intended as a simple guide to give you inspiration and advice on how to tone and strengthen any flabby muscles you have around the abs and buttocks. It will help you to achieve a well-toned, healthy body shape that will make you feel more confident.

But in order to succeed there are certain things that you need to spend time on each day.

Stretching

Greet each day with an early morning stretch either in or out of bed. Stress, watching TV and even lying in bed for 8 hours can all cause muscular aches and pains to develop.

This inactivity can ultimately lead to a build up of lactic acid in the muscles, resulting in pain and stiffness. That is why the daily routine of stretching the arms and body is invaluable.

Energy shower

There is nothing quite like an early morning energy shower to kick start the body into action so the first thing each morning jump into the shower and if brave enough, when you are ready to come out, turn the cold tap full on for several minutes.

After showering stimulate the body and boost the circulation by slapping the body all over. Using the flat of your hands, slap from toes to hips, wrists to shoulders and all over your chest, shoulders and torso before rubbing dry with a towel.

Little time to exercise today?

The various types of exercise recommended for toning and strengthening the abdominal area have already been discussed. Even if you haven't got much time to do a formal exercise session here are some ideas for activities that might just give you some inspiration.

Stand up and sit down: When you are in the house alone or having a long phone call with a friend, try this exercise for a total lower body workout. Stand up and sit down repeatedly between sets of leg crossing. It works like a squat to tone the thighs and bottom.

Deep breathing: There is nothing quite so invigorating or relaxing as 5 minutes of deep, steady breathing to shake away those cobwebs. Deep breathing is also excellent for helping to de-stress. Try it when alone:

• Sit in a quiet room.
• If you are wearing a skirt or trousers, undo the waistband so there is ample space for you to expand your tummy.
• Close your eyes, slowly breathe in, holding that breath to the count of five, and to the count of five slowly exhale through your mouth.
• Repeat again several times.

Meditation

Sit down in a room where there will be no distractions. If possible sit cross-legged on the floor.
• Now think of a simple sound to make, such as 'oo' or 'aah' – don't worry if it sounds silly, no-one else will hear.
• Repeat the sound out aloud. As you do so, try emptying your mind of any worries or concerns you may have – paying the bills, washing the curtains, what to cook for dinner. Stay focused on the sound you are making and nothing else but that sound.
• Continue repeating the sound for at least 5 minutes. Then sit quietly for a few minutes.
• You have had your first lesson in meditation. Now whenever you feel over-stressed or worried, try meditating. It's the perfect answer for helping relieve stress and improves the memory too!

Make sure that each day you:
✓ Have an early morning stretch
✓ Take a daily energy shower
✓ Spend 30 minutes exercising
✓ Build up a fitness routine with some stomach exercises
✓ Do some buttock exercises
✓ Take time to relax or better still, meditate
✓ Spend 5 minutes on quality breathing

Maintaining The Programme

Trying to change is never easy and there are bound to be occasions throughout the 28 days when you think why bother, what is the point of it all?

Remember why you initially embarked upon this programme and keep those aims and thoughts clearly focused in your mind. Write them down so you won't forget, tell your friends and family so that if you do happen to go off track they will be on hand to remind and help through.

It's often difficult to monitor your own progress but there are several things you can do before you start:

• Take your measurements around the buttocks, and waist and write them down on a chart.

• Weigh yourself (see the chart on page 183).

• Take a skirt or pair of trousers that are a little too snug around the midsection and aim that by the end of the programme you will be able to get into them comfortably.

But, most important of all, you should learn to respect and love yourself throughout this programme, pamper yourself with little treats, learn how to be good to yourself, after all you deserve it.

Have some fun

As children, having fun came naturally, but as adults we tend to forget how to have fun, and the more stressful and complex life becomes, the greater the need for the release that play provides. Having fun helps recharge our batteries so we can return to being an adult refreshed and ready for anything.

Look forward to something

Make sure that you always have something to look forward to. No matter how small or how insignificant it may appear, it's nice to have a simple treat in store.

Retail therapy

How about some fun shopping? If you feel in need of some pampering to keep your spirits up or if you have had a particularly bad day, why not go out and treat yourself to something. It must be the sheer excitement and thrill when you see a present to yourself being wrapped up that sends out the happy signals.

If you feel your life could do with an injection of fun, here's what to do:

• Once a week make time with friends or family to do something just for fun, rediscover a game or pastime you used to enjoy as a child but haven't done for a while, how about snakes and ladders, charades or rounders!

• Be creative – why not write a poem for a friend or a letter to your local newspaper.

• And try to laugh – it's the perfect de-stresser.

A summertime tan

There is no doubt that a slightly bronzed body looks healthier than a pale one and it gives the illusion of a slimmer outline too. But the health dangers related to exposure to the sun are well documented, so why not fake a tan? There are lots of good, easy-to-apply fake tan lotions to choose from in the shops.

Here are some fake tanning tips if, like many women, you find the biggest problem is applying the lotion without any telltale streaky lines:

• For the best results, exfoliate the skin and moisture it well at least an hour before applying the lotion.

• Pour some of the cream into the palm of one hand or onto a sponge mitten and massage it into your skin, spreading it evenly.

• Don't worry too much about the dry areas such as the elbows, knees and ankles, leave them until last because they often absorb too much colour.

• Two applications should suffice, the second application 3-4 hours after the first. By applying it this way you are building up the colour slowly for a truly natural look.

• Be sure to wait until the skin is completely dry before dressing.

• Fake tan can often stain the hands, so after using make sure that you clean your hands thoroughly with a nailbrush.

A pampering face mask

Having a facial at a beauty salon can be expensive and even buying some of the products can be costly, so why not make your own?

Sensitive skin: Blend half a cup of ground oatmeal with two teaspoons of water and four teaspoons of milk. Mix it into a paste and apply all over the face and neck. Leave for 10 minutes then gently wash off. Repeat once a week.

Dry skin: Mash up an avocado then apply to the face. Leave on for up to 15 minutes, then rinse. To be most effective, repeat once a week.

Oily skin; Beat one large egg white to make an oil-absorbing mask. Carefully apply to the face and leave until dry, then rinse well. Repeat twice a week to be most effective.

Posture practice

Good posture makes all the difference to the way an outfit hangs. It can make you appear slimmer and can also help prevent backache. Sitting with a slumped back and hunched shoulders is a position many of us adopt, particularly when stressed, tired or feeling self-conscious. If not remedied, it can ultimately result in a weakness developing in the stomach and back muscles.

• Try to keep your back straight, with shoulders and stomach pulled in and head held high, keeping chin parallel to the ground. Imagine there is a wire attached to the top of your head, holding you up.

• When bending to pick something up, we automatically bend our backs – this is wrong, always bend your knees and keep your back straight to help prevent back strain.

The Plan: Days 1–7

You've done all the preparatory work and so can look forward to the following 28-day plan in the knowledge that by the end you should feel invigorated and rejuvenated.

Whether you are a working woman or a busy mum, the next 28 days may mark the biggest change you are ever going to make in your life, so be prepared. Make up a chart and stick it on your kitchen wall so that you will remember what you must include each day in your programme.

If you can't decide on the exercise routine you want to do write them down each day and make up a chart alongside which you can record how many you achieved on that day. By doing this you will be able to keep a good detailed record account.

Here is a typical plan for day one but naturally times will differ depending on your home and work commitments and the order in which activities are done may also change according to your lifestyle.

7.15am Glass of hot water to which a squeeze of lemon or lime juice has been added. Stretch.

7.45am Early morning shower.

8.15am Breakfast – first day so choose something you are familiar with to ease you gently into the programme, perhaps cereal.

9.15am Clear away the breakfast things. Start on your exercise routine and spend time working on the abs this morning. Remember not to over-exert yourself and make sure that you do the warming up and cooling down routines.

10.15am Have a drink of water and do some quality breathing to compose yourself.

11.00am If it's a nice day why not go out for a brisk walk in the fresh air. If you've got a dog he's bound to

enjoy the longer than usual walk and if you don't have one surely there is a neighbour who would appreciate you taking out their canine friend.

1.00pm Time for lunch. A sandwich today with a piece of fruit and a glass of unsweetened fruit juice. Enjoy your lunch, this is your time to relax and savour what you are eating. After lunch sit down and listen to some music or watch the TV for a while.

3.00pm Back to some exercise, this time on the buttocks. Chose a routine with which you feel comfortable. Remember to warm up and cool down the body.

4.00pm Have a drink of cool, refreshing water and if you're alone in the house why not practise some meditation. It's a great way to unwind and get any niggling worries off your mind. You may well want to integrate this into your daily treatment.
6.00pm Time to prepare dinner – why not make a spaghetti bolognese?
7.00pm It has been an exhausting first day so you deserve a relaxing bath with some of your favourite essential oils and several candles creating a wonderfully soothing atmosphere.
8.00pm Watch a little TV or read a favourite book, snuggle up with your partner for a quiet chat and then why not have an early night.
Don't forget – as you complete each activity, tick it off on your chart and before you go to sleep remember to record in your diary how you felt, both the good and bad points. Plan what you intend doing the next day.

Remainder of the week

The remainder of week one should follow more or less the same basic routine but add in different foods and try different exercises. Don't try increasing the sit-ups or stomach exercises until the latter end of the week.

Bathtime paradise

Have a relaxing soak in the bath adding some favourite essential oils. **For a muscle soak:** sweet marjoram, black pepper and ginger all have a soothing and warming effect on aching sore muscles when added to the bath water.
Feeling in need of pampering: geranium, rose, ylang-ylang, jasmine, frankincense and sandalwood are all ideal for making you feel special. **Need reviving:** try adding grapefruit, rosemary and juniper to your bathwater.

Measurements chart

As you introduce exercise into your routine and reform your eating habits, you will find that not only are you toning up your hip, stomach and buttock muscles but you are looking good and feeling better. You have a new slimmer look and lots more energy!

You can record your measurements each week using this simple chart.

	Week 1	Week 2	Week 3	Week 4
Date				
Weight				
Bust				
Waist				
Hips				
Thighs				

The Plan: Days 8–14

With the first week over, you're bound to have developed certain routines now and are hopefully learning to make your meals more exciting.

If you have been exercising correctly you should be feeling some of the results of your hard work and be pushing yourself a little further.

7.15am Glass of hot water and lime juice. Stretch.
7.45am Early morning shower.
8.15am Breakfast – treat yourself to some home-made muesli.

9.15am Why not do some gardening today in place of 30 minutes exercise.
10.15am Make yourself a refreshing herbal tea. Then sit down and play some favourite music, don't worry if you fall asleep, just enjoy this half-hour of peace and tranquillity.

11.00am Time for some gentle exercise for the buttocks.
1.00pm Time for lunch. All that exercising has brought on an appetite so have a jacket potato with some baked beans and chilli powder. Finish off with a refreshing glass of unsweetened apple juice, then tackle some housework.
3.00pm It's back to some exercise, this time on the stomach. Chose a routine with which you feel comfortable. Remember to warm up and cool down the body.
4.00pm Have a cool drink of water and, if you're alone in the house, why not practise some DIY reflexology to help eliminate any stress and tension.
6.00pm Time to prepare dinner – for simplicity, tonight why not make pasta.
7.00pm Give your nails a manicure – they'll need it after all the gardening.
8.00pm Do some quality breathing and why not practise some good posture moves, ideal for keeping those flabby stomach muscles in check, making you look slimmer and feel more confident too.

Don't forget – check each activity off on your chart as you do it and write up your diary at the end of each day.

Remainder of the week

The remainder of week two should follow more or less the same basic routine, but be sure to try different exercises and food – don't let boredom set in.

The Plan: Days 15–21

You will by now have established a daily eating and exercising routine and perhaps made some changes. So are you ready for week three?

7.15am Have a glass of hot water with lemon juice. Do a variety of stretching exercises. Try this super back stretch: Kneel on the floor and then sit back on to your heels. Fold forward with your arms outstretched in front you until your forehead reaches the floor. Rest your face on a cushion if you cannot comfortably reach the floor.

7.45am Early morning shower.

8.15am Breakfast – have something warm, perhaps a muffin.

9.15am Do the full workout on the stomach and buttocks.

10.15am Pop out to the shops and have some retail therapy, but leave the car at home and walk. Treat yourself to a new T-shirt or blouse, then stop in a café for a cup of herbal tea. Why not call into the library on your way home and choose a music disc or comedy video to borrow.

12.00pm Do some quality breathing.

1.00pm Time for lunch. Have a sandwich and an orange.

3.00pm You enrolled this week for a few sessions down at the local gym to work out on their pieces of equipment. Make sure that you have a word with one of the fitness experts on duty so they can show you exactly what to do.

5.00pm Make yourself a cup of herbal tea, put on some music and relax.

6.00pm Time to prepare dinner – how about a chicken dish tonight with brown rice.

7.00pm Give yourself a face mask.

8.00pm Run a relaxing bath and soak in it whilst burning some relaxing essential oils such as lavender or geranium. Light a few candles to set the scene and as the bath water runs in add your favourite aromatherapy bath oil.

Don't forget – check each activity off on your chart as you do it and write up your diary at the end of each day.

Remainder of the week

It's nearly the end of your programme and by now you will probably be feeling more energetic and slightly more confident in your appearance, but don't give up. You have another seven days to go. It's still not too late to take up another activity or enrol in a class at the local gym.

The Plan: Days 22–28

This is it, the final week. Are you ready for whatever lies in store? And if you need reminding, get those trousers out from the wardrobe and see how they fit you now.

7.15am Glass of hot water with lime juice. Stretch.

7.45am Early morning shower.

8.15am Breakfast. Have cereal this morning with a low-fat yogurt

9.15am Time for some brisk power walking. This time you should be able to go further than you did in the first few weeks and when you arrive back home you shouldn't feel so exhausted.

10.15am Why not prepare the ingredients for lunch and whilst doing practise some buttock squeezing exercises – never waste a moment! Sit down and have a glass of water or herbal tea and take time to look back over your diary and chart your progress,

11.00am Time for a housework blitz and if you don't really feel in the mood, just imagine how many calories you will be burning up.

1.00pm Time for lunch. Invite a friend round so prepare jacket potatoes with some special toppings and a glass of apple juice each.

3.00pm Now is the time to do your full abs and buttock workout. You should used to the exercises now so why not play some music in the background.

4.00pm No need to prepare any tea because you are going out for dinner this evening so why

not spend time applying fake tan – not only will it make you look healthier but you will feel pretty good too, especially as friends have been remarking on how trim you now look.

6.00pm Get ready for your evening out, have a glass of water and perhaps some grapes to stave off the hunger pangs before going out.

7.00pm In the restaurant remember to choose your meal wisely. Keep away from creamy or deep-fried dishes. And to celebrate your evening, have a glass of wine.

10.00pm After such a special day, have an early night. Getting sufficient sleep is just as important as all the exercising and healthy eating.

Don't forget to measure your waist and buttocks and then check where there has been some reduction. See if you can wriggle into that skirt or those tight jeans that have been torturing you for the last 12 months and then, if you must, hop on to the scales.

Remainder of the week

Keep up with the routine even to the very last day. And when the final day arrives you can heave a sigh of relief and give yourself a huge hug – you've done it.

Activity Record Chart

Record your activities every day using this table

DAILY ACTIVITIES	1	2	3	4	5	6	7	8	9	10	11	12	13	14	15	16	17	18	19	20	21	22	23	24	25	26	27	28
Early morning stretch																												
Glass of hot water and lemon or lime juice																												
Daily energy shower																												
Breakfast																												
Lunch																												
Dinner																												
175g (6oz) protein food																												
350g (12oz) fresh fruit/juice																												
175g (6oz) bread, cereal etc																												
450ml ($^3/_4$ pint) semi-skimmed or skimmed milk																												
1.75 litres (3 pints) water																												
30 mins exercise																												
Stomach exercise routine																												
Buttock exercise routine																												
5 mins quality breathing																												

Congratulations!

Provided you have followed the programme and undertaken the exercises as recommended, not slipped off the bandwagon and given yourself too many 'treats', your hard work should have paid off with a well-toned, healthy stomach and firmer buttocks.

Don't worry if you still have a little way to go to achieve that sylph-like figure you have long dreamed of – remember everyone's metabolism is different and you've done really well to get this far.

To maintain your new look:
- Continue eating three meals a day.
- Try sticking to low-fat foods.
- Continue taking regular aerobic exercise.
- Remember good posture is important.
- Don't become obsessive about your weight, after all your aim was to tone and strengthen your stomach muscles and now you have achieved that you can be pretty proud of yourself
- Enjoy your new shape.

Dining out
Some tips for when you go out for a delicious meal at the end of the programme to celebrate your success.

Italian Choose pasta with vegetables or with tomato or seafood sauce
- Pizzas are okay provided they have a thin crust
- Say no to cream or cheese-based sauces and oil salad dressings.

Chinese Choose steamed and stir-fried dishes
- Plain boiled rice and noodles have far fewer calories than special or egg fried rice
- Go for prawns or chicken instead of beef or duck

- Say no to sweet and sour dishes or ones with thick sauces.

Indian Boiled rice, naan and chapattis are far better than oily paratha bread
- Tandooris, dry curries and tikkas are fine too
- Say no to deep fried bhajis, samosas and creamy kormas.

English Choose skinless chicken, served with a jacket potato or, better still, a green side salad
- Opt for grilled or steamed white fish served with a selection of fresh vegetables
- Avoid pies
- Say no to fish and chips.

The 28 Day Plan Notebook